The Curmudgeon Speaks!

Also by Fred Weissman:

Great Soup . Can I Have The Recipe?,
with co-author Barbara Johnson Weissman

The Curmudgeon Speaks!

The Complete Collection of his finest short works,

encompassing Reflections, Homespun Wisdom,

Humor, Musings, Nostalgia, Reminiscences, Ironies,

Witticisms, Oddities, Sarcasms, Appreciations,

Attitudes, Insights, Things to Think About

and Some Well-Intended Advice.

by Fred Weissman

Order this book online at www.trafford.com
or email orders@trafford.com

Most Trafford titles are also available at major online book retailers.

Note for Librarians: A cataloguing record for this book is available from Library
and Archives Canada at www.collectionscanada.ca/amicus/index-e.html

Printed in Victoria, BC, Canada.

ISBN: 978-1-4269-2045-5 (sc)

ISBN: 978-1-4269-2046-2 (dj)

LIBRARY OF CONGRESS CONTROL NUMBER: 2009939380

*Our mission is to efficiently provide the world's finest, most comprehensive book publishing
service, enabling every author to experience success. To find out how to publish your book, your
way, and have it available worldwide, visit us online at www.trafford.com*

Trafford rev. 12/15/2009

 www.trafford.com

North America & international
toll-free: 1 888 232 4444 (USA & Canada)
phone: 250 383 6864 ♦ fax: 812 355 4082

Preface

You're going to like this book—maybe not every single item in it, but there are more than enough subjects to share with you in an enjoyable, interesting and, for the most part, positive way. Many involve suggestions, advice or unusual experiences (all original at the time, to the best of my knowledge). Some may be addressed more strongly but most are not controversial and are expressed with anything from humor to sarcasm. This is exactly why curmudgeons are important: we try to be helpful without being scathing.

How many times have you read an editorial or article presenting a particular point of view on a troublesome subject, at the end of which you announce, *"That's bull crap! He's got that completely backwards!"*? How often have you spoken out about a trend that's bothered you for some time, and been ignored, only to have the nation suddenly become aware of it when someone more famous than you expresses an opinion about it on television, and all you can do is blurt out, with some frustration, *"Oh, come on! I've been saying the same thing for years!"*? Well, welcome to the club.

I don't know if "curmudgeon" is the right word for us. Some older dictionaries defined us as "irascible" and "churlish"; newer ones tone it down to "crusty" and "ill-tempered" and "usually old." Crusty, maybe; old, probably, but ill-tempered or nasty, no. I see us as individuals aware of issues but, even more important, of trends or directions towards which our country has been heading that could be detrimental if allowed to continue unchecked. Aware of some negative trends for decades, we've been able to see the extent of change over time, evaluate the results and alert others to what we perceive so that perhaps they'll become concerned. In some ways that makes us seers or sentinels.

We also have other attributes that we try to put to good use. In fact, in many respects, we're probably like you in a lot of positive ways. It's just that we're older, have had more time to observe and get involved, and no longer have to worry about losing our jobs.

All told, maybe it's these qualities that make curmudgeons our nation's best hope for continued successful independent survival.

Cuddebackville
May, 2008

Contents

The Curmudgeon Speaks!

Chapter 1 –

Where Is Henry Higgins When We Need Him?

In *"My Fair Lady,"* which was both a play and a movie, Rex Harrison is Professor Henry Higgins, an "expert dialectician and grammarian" who deplores the decline in the quality of speech in England. Asking "Why Can't the English Teach Their Children How to Speak," he notes that other nations continue to maintain their language learning skills; just English is threatened. His only comfort comes when he observes that "there even are places where English completely disappears (in America, they haven't used it for years!)." He may have been right; please read on.

Closure

I was driving one day, listening to an all-news radio station, when the time came for their every-eight-minutes traffic and weather update. The alert helicopter pilot reported a serious accident on a major highway, resulting in "the closure of two lanes of traffic on the westbound side." Other pilots, along with media news personalities, quickly picked up on the *mot nouvelle* and began using the suddenly trendy word in their traffic reports.

"Closure?"

Technically, perhaps it's correct, but the word has been used for many decades to describe the peace and comfort that come with the resolution of an upsetting, long-term situation to those who have suffered with it. Closure is achieved when the pervert who raped and killed a family's nine-year-old child is finally apprehended, tried and convicted for life, with no chance for parole; it should not be used to describe a ramp shutdown on the New Jersey Turnpike.

I think most media personnel will consider this and agree to return to the use of the more familiar and descriptive "closing," for which I thank you here in advance.

But to those insensitive few who reject my recommendation and insist on promoting inappropriate and unnecessary new uses for existing words, I have a suggestion: perhaps you should just closure mouths and let the others do the traffic reports.

Cool, Awesome And, Uh, Like, Y'know, Like

Many words have multiple meanings, even when used as only one part of speech, such as an adjective. Often, those meanings increase to accommodate trendy or current descriptive extremes or circumstances. This can be good; such dynamism is probably one element that keeps a language vibrant and alive. "Cool," for example, certainly describes more than just the weather outside or a dispassionate greeting. Some forms of jazz have a certain suave, sophisticated style that has been described as "cool" for decades. And how many of us wouldn't welcome an opportunity to win a "cool" hundred-million-dollar lottery? That's cool.

A new use for a word can be welcome, but not if that use is to cover up a lack of verbal skills, knowledge or vocabulary. The uniqueness of that word's descriptive quality then becomes lost. In that context, these omnipresent examples come to mind.

The first just happens to involve the word "cool" itself. The simplest, most insignificant event is cool; everything is cool.

"It was 103 degrees here yesterday, and our neighbor's house was on fire."

"Cool."

"The kitchen sink overflowed."

"Cool."

Of course, whatever isn't cool simply has to be awesome.

"I was raking leaves, and saw a penny on the lawn."

"Cool."

"I bent down to pick it up, and guess what? It was a dime!"

"Awesome!"

"I just bought three new pairs of socks—they were on sale."

"Awesome!"

Everybody pauses in mid-sentence occasionally. A creative thought, impromptu statement or delicate response to a question can elicit an occasional pause punctuated by an "um-mm" or "uh." The further inclusion of the word "like," however (often paired with "y'know"), may be the best indicator of an inability to form even a simple complete sentence when speaking. "I'm, uh, like, y'know, goin' to, y'know, the store to, uh, like, buy two or three bags of, y'know, pretzels." Sounds like it's time to get off the Internet and rediscover analog communication—speech.

It's All Right—Now You Can Be Empathetic

Until a few years ago, if you sympathized with or expressed sympathy for a person, you were said to be sympathetic. However, if you empathized with or expressed empathy for a person, you were said to be empathic. Strangely, there was no such word as "empathetic," even though common sense and the already-established "sympathetic" should have dictated that as the obvious choice. Well, probably due to repeated (although erroneous) use of that nonexistent word, it became legitimate and acceptable, so that no longer do you have to be merely empathic, you can now stretch your emotions and be fully empathetic.

Why You Cannot Graduate From College

You work hard for years in college, perhaps even attending at night while holding down a full-time job. Finally, you receive that coveted academic degree in your area of specialization. You earned it, and are now a college graduate.

But you didn't graduate; you *were graduated.* It was the college who rewarded and finalized your good efforts, and that's the key: whether or not you can control the outcome of a situation.

"Graduate," used in its intransitive form, seems to be the only verb misused in this manner. "I graduated high school last year" or "Next year I graduate college" are used commonly; yet you never hear a child say, "I promoted to seventh grade;" he *was promoted.* Similarly, an employee can promote an idea, but *is promoted* at work. One *is divorced,* or *was married.*

He can die, but if it's the result of violence, he *was killed*. Your daughter *is born*—it's mom who completes the nine-month process.

And someday she'll apply to a few colleges and select one to attend, but only if she *is accepted* by that institution.

Of Course, Assume And Generalize

There's a saying, "Never assume; it makes an A-S-S out of U and M-E." Cute, but people quote it seriously and mean it.

They shouldn't; life is based on assumptions. We encounter a situation and almost instinctively analyze it and form an opinion. We see a continuing future that includes us as participants. It is that optimism which lets us make dinner reservations for next Friday, or buy season tickets to the Yankee games, which are months away, or plan now for next year's vacation. It's why we try to save some of our job pay for our kids' education and our own retirement, each of which demands enormous amounts of money.

I plan to mow the lawn tomorrow, but they're predicting rain. If they're right, maybe I'll update my resumé instead.

"You can't generalize" is another unforgiving generalization that is unnecessarily uncompromising. You can generalize, but to make it acceptable, base it solely on personal experience. Be a verbal artist and create an attention-getting miniature instead of a broad sweeping mural. If you travel below the Mason-Dixon Line and find the drawl of most Southerners charming, fine—that's a basis for making a generalization. But don't categorize all Martians as being little green creatures with huge heads if you've never even seen one.

I was going to say we all generalize, but that's an assumption. I guess it's better to say we all make assumptions, even though that's a generalization.

Why Do Homosexuals Have To Be Gay?

I have absolutely no problem with anybody's sexual orientation. Many renowned people throughout history have been homosexuals, especially in the arts. This does not make their accomplishments any less impressive or enjoyable. The music of Tchaikovsky, for example, will always be loved and performed, and should be.

However, I do have one thing against all homosexuals: why couldn't they remain queer? Why did they have to become gay?

"Gay" used to be a word whose use brought to mind an image of something or someone delightful, happy, cheerful, exuberant or lively. The theme at a party could be described as "gay;" so could the mood of the people at that party. Movie titles such as "Our Hearts Were Young and Gay" evoked pleasant sentiments. Now, even I find myself suppressing a bemused smile when I see "The Gay Divorcée" scheduled to be shown on TV, or hear that line from "Deck The Halls" that goes, "Don we now our gay apparel."

I'm Afraid You've Got That Backward

Three common examples of putting the cart before the horse:
1) "Back and forth" —Everybody says it, usually with varying degrees of exasperation. "All day long I've been running back and forth, back and forth." The thing is, how can you come back before you've gone forth?
2) "Coming and going" —Similarly, you have to go before you can come back.
3) "Hit and run" —When describing an automobile accident, "hit and run" is fine, but not in baseball. When you have a runner on first base, and he breaks for second as the pitcher releases the ball toward home plate, this is "run and hit"—even though everyone calls it a "hit and run play," or notes that "the hit and run was on." Why? What is so difficult about "run and hit?"

This Is So-o-o-o-o Fun!

Getting together with friends on July 4th for an outdoor party is *such fun!* The weather cooperates, the barbecued goodies are ample and many of their jokes, as always, are *so funny.* The kids have *much fun* playing ball, and the time flies by. Everyone has *fun*, and all agree that it really was a *fun* day.

That's *funny*, though—not even one child thought that it was *so fun.* Now *how fun* is that?

Say That Again?

"Reiterate" is another commonly misused word, by at least one degree of repetition.

When one expresses an opinion, idea or thought, he makes a statement. If that statement is repeated for emphasis or any other reason, it is iterated. Make the same point a third time, and it has been reiterated. So if someone says, "Let me again reiterate," he is preparing you to hear that statement for yet a fourth time.

Are You On Line Or In Line?

People used to claim they could tell where in the nation you came from by whether you said you were going to get "on line" or "in line" to buy something such as theatre tickets. Actually, it has nothing to do with being some sort of regional or idiomatic expression; it's merely a matter of descriptive accuracy.

If there is a line of people waiting for the box office to open up, and you join them as the last person in the queue, then you are "on line." If you are there with a companion, and you both walk back to the end of the line and become part of it, both of you are "on line." Then, after awhile, let's say your companion gets tired of waiting and wants to check out an item of clothing in a store window just down the block. She says she'll be back in a bit and would you hold her place? Of course, you say, and off she goes. Moments later she's back, and rejoins the line. At this point, if there's still nobody behind, she has gotten back "on line;" but if others have arrived and added to the length of the waiting line, then she has "cut in" or gotten back "in line."

An interesting footnote: my wife and I attended a wedding. The food at the reception was served buffet-style from a row of tables at the front end of the room. Soon, the guests were invited to come up and help themselves to the goodies. We were seated in the back, and I didn't want to wait half an hour to eat, so I got up and got "on line." Looking back, I saw my wife still chatting with friends at our table, so I called out, "Honey, come on! We have to get on line!" The lady ahead of me turned, looked me over and asked, seriously, "You brought your computer along?"

But It's Not Pronounced That Way

It's astonishing (but not surprising) how many words are not pronounced properly or have the wrong syllable emphasized (in the old days, we jokingly mispronounced the word "syllable" as "syl-LAH-ble," accenting the second syllable). There are many examples of these two types of incorrect pronunciation, some of which are presented here for your consideration.

❑ The phrase is "preventive medicine," not "preven*ta*tive medicine." The word is "preventive," *not* "preven*ta*tive."

❑ In England, you can wear jew-ELLERY; in our country, however, wear "JEW-el-ree;" "JEW-*leree*" is *so* not with it.

❑ A hurricane can cause "ir-REV-ocable" damage, but *never* "irre-VOC-able" damage. It's true that correct pronunciation of a word can be a "FOR-midable" challenge, but *never* a "for-MID-able" one. Similarly, in certain situations, "APP-licable" rules may apply, but *never* "a PLICK-able" ones.

❏ One day in the late 1980s I was listening to WQXR, a New York City classical music radio station. A reasonably familiar and well-known selection was being played, and when it ended, the announcer informed us that what we had just heard was a performance of "Johann Sebastian Bach's 'TOE-cuh-TAH and Fugue in D Minor'." I couldn't believe it—an announcer on one of the most *hauteur* stations in the country didn't know the piece, much less that the word was pronounced "toe-CAH-tah."

❏ Here are some goodies: Lincoln's Birthday is in Feb*ru*ary, *not* "Febuary;" by the time you have become a college graduate, you should have received a good "*ed-u*-CA-shun," *not* an "edge-ih-CA-shun;" if you want to start your own *bizzness*, that's better than going into "*bidness*" or "*binness*." And by the way, did you know that the preferred pronunciation for an oven used to make pottery is "kill," even though the word is spelled "kiln?"

❏ Everyone uses measurements; they're a basic part of our multi-dimensional world. How wide is that parking space? How tall is she? Although four common words are used in answers, only three—length, width and depth—are pronounced properly. The fourth one—height—often is mispronounced as "*heidth.*"

❏ Recent President George W. Bush and others pronounce the word "nuclear" as if it were spelled "nuc*ular*." Years ago, though, when we visited the Catawba Nuclear Power Plant near Rock Hill, South Carolina, we were surprised and somewhat disappointed to hear most of the announcers on the various recorded video displays also using the "nuc*ular*" pronunciation.

Be Careful Of Having An Apostrophic Stroke

In a rather upscale shopping mall in southeastern Florida, a sign in the window of one establishment announced, "Visitor's Welcome." In lower New York State, a Greek-style diner with two restrooms identified one as being for "Gentlemen" and the other as being for "Ladie's." A notice outside a church in Iowa urged congregants to attend Sunday morning services and learn more about "Gods' Will." A used car ad in a Sunday newspaper stated the vehicle "Run's and look's great. Everything work's."

These are just four examples of apostrophically-challenged signage. We've all seen some, whether it was one announcing a sale on "Pajama's" or another urging town residents to "Vote Yes for Higher Pay for Teacher's." The solution is easy: just let plural be plural instead of possessive.

The most common mistake? Probably the use of "its." When written "it's," that makes it a contraction meaning either "it is" or "it has;" otherwise, no apostrophe is needed—it's that simple.

Delicious Mushrooms That Cast A Spell

No matter how you slice it, properly prepared mushrooms are a treat. One of the best-tasting yet affordable varieties includes the Portobello, especially in soups that call for fresh mushrooms. They are quite flexible in culinary use and, oddly, in spelling as well. We've seen the word typically spelled in any one of three ways: "Port*a*bell*a*," "Port*a*bell*o*" and "Port*o*bell*a*." It's unusual, though, to see it spelled properly, which still is "Port*o*bell*o*."

Now you may feel that I'm being too nit-picky, but spelling is important. Imagine how awkward or embarrassing it could be if mushroom type "Shiitake" was spelled with only one "i."

Impress Your Friends With Even More Trivia

It's always amusing to hear someone described as a glutton because "he eats like a horse" or, conversely, as a sensible eater because "she eats like a bird." A horse eats less than one-fourth of its body weight per day; a bird consumes over three times its body weight each day. So much for well-intended compliments.

When something is to be divided between at least two people, and one gets a considerably larger portion than anyone else, that person is said to have received "the lion's share," implying that he or she received the majority, if not most, of the take. But did you know that "the lion's share" means he or she received it *all*?

When ownership of an item is in dispute, whoever has actual possession of it at the moment may try to strengthen his or her claim by using the familiar phrase, "Possession is nine-tenths of the law." It's impressive and convincing, but the true expression is, "Possession is nine *points* of the law."

There is another familiar expression that is often misquoted when used, but the funny thing is, it works either way. Someone will opine that "Music hath charms to soothe the savage beast," which evokes a totally credible, plausible mental image; yet the actual expression is, "Music hath charms to soothe the savage *breast*." It's probably more esoteric, but in truth I actually prefer the use of the first one.

Sometimes a person will reach a conclusion, make a decision or express an opinion about an issue based on scant information, which might be inaccurate or, at best, include only part of the entire picture. It can be a foolish or even dangerous thing to do, which is why many have noted that "A little knowledge is a dangerous thing," quoting a line written by Alexander Pope. It's an apt reference, but inaccurate; what Pope actually wrote was, "A little *learning* is a dangerous thing."

Some movie buffs may remember a movie made in 1968 or 1969 entitled, "Krakatoa East of Java," starring the incomparable Maximilian Schell. I imagine that some research and effort went into its creation and production, yet the most obvious item seems to have been totally overlooked: Krakatoa is *west* of Java.

Chapter 2 –

Some Homespun Wisdom, Humor, Reflections And Musings

Some original observations (as far as I know) that my wife Barbara and I formulated over the years which we hope will help you throughout life (or at least amuse you):

1) A watched pot never boils, but it allows you to raise the stovetop heat so that eventually it will.
2) The hardest part of a thousand-mile journey is the first 998 miles; the rest, you can walk.
3) Flattery is the sincerest form of insincerity.
4) You know you're getting old when family gets together for the Passover Seder—and it's at your home.
5) Do Lipton Tea employees ever get a coffee break?
6) Does any worker at Morton or Diamond Crystal ever end lunch hour with, "Well, back to the salt mines."?
7) We all have time for those things for which we choose to make time.
8) To help find a needle in a haystack, use a magnet.
9) Skim milk comes from cows that graze on Astroturf.
10) No matter where we go on vacation, the area seems to be populated by locals.

11) It's tough to get going in the morning without coffee, which is why it's tough to make coffee in the morning.

12) I have nothing against any child psychologist but I'd rather confide in an adult.

13) How clever of the Lord to create national parks so close to already-existing major roads!

14) If train travel affords you vistas and scenery unmatched by other conventional means, why do their brochures, ads and documentaries show these breathtaking views from an angle taken above the train from an airplane?

15) Travel ads in magazines, newspapers, pamphlets and brochures always contain alluring, irresistible shots of scenery—mountains, valleys, beaches, area attractions or historical architecture that you, too, can experience on your next vacation. The problem is, how many of these depictions include the fog, rain or dreary overcast conditions that will probably be there on *your* visit?

16) How do people who can't see without their glasses find them when they've forgotten where they left them?

17) A soup recipe said to combine all ingredients in a pot and bring to a boil, which I did. It then said to simmer, partially covered, for 45 minutes, so I took my pants off. I can't say the soup tasted any better for doing it.

18) Weissman's Law: To find the diameter of any given irregular solid, simply multiply the radius by two.

19) The Weissman-Zar Law of Research Inconsistencies: Where the several documents conflict, the most inaccurate should be regarded as the least reliable.

20) There is a saying, "Let sleeping dogs lie." The problem, sadly, is that we all know a few sleeping dogs, and they'll lie whether you let them or not.

21) With good people, what you see is what you get; with others, what you don't see is what you get.

22) An Episcopalian can be thought of as an "R.C. Lite": no Pope, and one-third the saints.

23) All toothless people should be indentured.

24) I never married my wife because of her taste in men.

25) No environmentalist I've ever known would vote for a Republican for President.

26) When someone is telling a joke, enjoy it, and try not to anticipate the punch line. After all, it's just a joke, not a riddle or a murder mystery.

27) One advantage of having money is that you can indulge in conspicuous consumption, but an even greater benefit is that you don't have to.

28) Do vegetarians perform oral sex?

29) It is music that is the universal language. Math never was, and never will be.

30) When a person says, "Can I ask you a question?", he already has.

31) When inquiring about someone's health or how things are going, listening to the tone of the responder's voice over the telephone will tell you far more than any response you'll read over the Internet.

Waitresses In Chinese Buffet Restaurants

There are people who love Chinese food but want it served to them at their table, so they go to a regular Chinese restaurant for a meal. Most people, though, I think prefer buffet style because it has variety; you can eat as much as you like of whatever you like. Either way, you are attended to and surrounded by a staff of helpers of both sexes, most of whom are waitresses.

Have you ever really looked closely at them? It's amazing. Almost without exception, it seems that no waitress has a waist larger than 19 inches or weighs more than 97 pounds.

How in hell do they do it? If I worked in a Chinese buffet-style eatery, I know I'd gain 100 pounds in a month (assuming they didn't fire me for snacking after one week). Either Chinese women have great willpower, or they have generously shared with us the hidden value of chopsticks—namely, that you can't pig out as quickly with them as you can with a fork and knife.

Guess I'll just have to suffer myself to settle for a job behind the counter at a Jewish delicatessen. Of course, it will only be a temporary position.

Two Good Tips For You To Consider

Speaking of dining establishments that offer "all you can eat" buffets (sometimes along with full-service dinners), many people who opt for this choice leave less of a tip because they feel that since they are getting their own food, they are effectively serving themselves. So if a 15% tip is traditional for full-meal service, 10% is acceptable for buffet service.

But think about that for a moment. Sure, you went up to the food area and filled your own plate with selections that appealed to you, brought them back to your table, and feasted. Then you probably returned to enjoy a second round of different choices—and maybe even for a third round—before going one last time to finish up with a few delicious desserts.

And during that entire time, who removed your bowls, plates and napkins throughout each stage? Who frequently refilled the pitcher, cups or glasses? Who helped make sure that your needs were met, including checking the status of the food trays?

This is why we tip good waiters and waitresses at least 15%, whether we're at a full-service or "self-service" establishment.

Which brings me to the second tip: if your waiter or waitress has performed in an especially outstanding, cheerful or pleasant manner (particularly under pressure), please increase the tip to 20%. They've earned it, and deserve it. More significantly, you would be amazed (and perhaps distressed) to learn how badly that extra money is needed by waitresses for whom this is but one of two full-time jobs, or by a waiter for whom this evening work is in addition to his full-time college attendance. I have to believe that the five per cent difference is not a burden, and we can assure you from numerous experiences nationwide that in too many cases, the money is critical to the recipient.

Proverbial Conflicts

On the one hand, "Haste makes waste;" then again, "He who hesitates is lost." Apparently, if the shoe doesn't fit, adjust it.

How To Segregate Kibitzers

Typically, a "kibitzer" is one who observes some form of card game being played and offers unsolicited comments or advice. While there are two acceptable ways to pronounce the word, Jews usually like to *kib*itz; non-Jews ask if they can kib*itz*.

The Neighborhood Watch

A lot of people in our town may be poor, but we do have a neighborhood watch.

And this month it's my turn to wear it.

The Funniest Joke I've Heard In Years

Your taxes are going down next year.

I Was A Poet And Didn't Know It

In the last year of grade school, many classmates included a poem when they signed your autograph book. It usually began "Roses are red, violets are blue" and concluded with sentiments ranging from "Sugar is sweet and so are you" to "If I looked like you I'd live in a zoo."

Silly, but hey, we were kids; besides, they rhymed and had rhythm, enabling them to be recited in that unmistakable sing-song style of narration that, after awhile, we grew to dislike.

That year, an unusually hot and dry June slowly changed the grasses at our upstate summer place to a flaxen-tan color, which persisted through the season. One morning, sitting on the front deck rereading the new entries in my autograph book, I looked up and happened to see the lawn in sunlight. The lack of nearly any green color was startling. That, paired with those annoying verses I was perusing in the book, created a thought which, of course, had to be expressed in a rebellious form. And that is how, at the age of eleven, I wrote my first poem:

Roses are red,
Violets are blue.
Grass is green except in the summer when,
Due to lack of water, it turns brown and dies.

It didn't take long to realize that the selection probably would not compete with anything Walt Whitman had devised because when I recited or showed it to people, they assured me that it was cute, even funny, but certainly not poetry. It didn't *rhyme*, and poetry simply *had* to rhyme. Crushed, I buried my crude attempt to describe a scene in a simple but inelegant manner and forgot about it until the late 1990s.

Reading the poems included in a review of a newly-published contemporary collection in *"The New York Times"* Book Review one Sunday, along with the "poems" in several issues of *"The New Yorker"* magazine over the next three months made me realize that some fifty years earlier I had inadvertently created what is now referred to as "modern poetry." Forget rhyme (or reason); what used to be called "a narrative" or "prose" or a combination of both was now being identified as "poetry." All one had to do was write several sentences in an inexplicable arrangement of lines that visually imitated a verse or stanza, and it was revered as a poem. I couldn't find one with even a pretense of cadence or meter, never mind a mellifluous or euphonious quality when read aloud. How, why and when did this transition take place? Good grief! At this rate, anything is creative poetry—to wit:

The Storm

She walked slowly, with an almost imperceptible
Limp that belied the pained look on her face.
The bag secured by her left arm pressed against her

    Bosom in the manner of a child,
    Except that it was much heavier
        And refused to squirm.
    The house was now far behind her, and
    Only the beckoning road ahead seemed
        To command her attention.

The distant thunder electrified her into quickening
Her pace, finally reaching the road at path's end
At which a colorful conical cylindrical container
Awaited. Staring ahead at the ominous, darkening
Clouds, she extended her occupied arm towards them,
Releasing the burdensome bag. It struck the receptacle
And, for just an instant, balanced there, as if waiting for
Instructions, then leaned to the right and fainted, its
Contents tumbling earthward along with the first few
Drops of rain—thunder's cloudy promise fulfilled!

    Watching this, my heart started to ache
    For her until I realized that this couldn't
    Be the first time she had taken out the
    Garbage. Didn't she know that first you
    Have to take the lid off the garbage can?

Sentiments can also be expressed in the form of haiku:

    Poetry, to me,
    Has lines that not only rhyme
    But exude rhythm.

If that's not trendy or artsy enough, I proffer tanka:

    I just can't believe
    That the narrative nonsense
    Being penned today
    Is considered poetry.
    We used to call this stuff prose.

Well, enough said; time to move ahead.

The Birth Of The Piano

Listen for just one hour to any live or recorded performance of several Bach Toccatas and Fugues being played solely on a harpsichord, and you will understand why God, in His infinite wisdom and mercy, quietly guided the development of the piano.

Needed: Better Hurricane Management

Recently, during an unexpectedly brutal hurricane season in southern Florida, the Governor ordered almost one million local residents to evacuate immediately. They did, and the resulting stench was unbearable.

You Can't See Everything When Travelling

The best part of a vacation trip or tour is enjoying what you experience. This seems elementary, but let's face it, no matter where you go or how long you stay there, you can't see and do everything, and sure enough, when you return, there will always be someone who will ask, "Ah, you went to Schvitzenfartzen? Did you see the Windbeutel Museum and take a tour?" And, of course, you will not have. But did that person take the left turn off the highway like you did to explore that compelling, nearly irresistible side road that gave you unparalleled views of the mountains while taking you through some of the loveliest valleys and hillside villages in that part of the country? And did he get to enjoy that small, charming restaurant you came across on that detour, the one whose scenic views and homemade specialties made your meal one of the best of the entire trip? Did he get to tour the local museum? I doubt it—but you did. What a day!

Cabin Fever

Winter is a tough time of year in the northern part of the United States, especially for retired people. So often we hear of friends and neighbors who "just can't stand being cooped up."

For these people, here's a thought: there are many things you can do that will not only alleviate boredom but will also add to the quality of your life. Let me suggest just two.

One involves volunteering. Do you know how desperately our country needs people to give freely and generously of their time to help worthy causes? You could help serve or prepare food for a meal at your local house of worship, work with area youth groups, be a docent at a local museum, serve on your town council, or at least attend and participate in meetings, train others in some field in which you have expertise, help to catalog and document photos or other items for an historical society—the list is endless. Any amount of time you can give as a volunteer will matter, and most places value such selfless contributions. Just as important, though, you will experience an inner satisfaction and gratification that no amount of money in the world can ever provide. Believe me, you have to volunteer to do something you truly want to be involved with to fully understand the feeling. And, as an added bonus, if you're retired, it's a wonderful way to "give something back" to the community.

If that involves too much time or commitment, what about a creative activity you can do at home? For example, try to cook or bake specialties that you like. Learn how to draw or paint, or play a musical instrument. Come to think of it, why not write a book, or a series of short stories or articles? After all, yours is a unique life. How old are you, and where did you live and grow up? What have you experienced that is unusual, perhaps unique, that is worth sharing from your perspective? What changes or trends over the years have pleased you or caused you concern? How about some noteworthy people or events in your life? The possibilities are mind-boggling, but what an opportunity to share your ideas, opinions and adventures with us in your own words and style. And that's so much better than just looking forward to spring.

Chapter 3 –

It Pays To Shop Smart

Too many people underestimate the importance and value of knowing how to shop for everyday items, particularly at grocery stores or supermarkets. They totally ignore circulars that come either in the mail or in the Sunday newspaper. "I don't have the time to do comparison shopping or check out the circulars." "I'm not running all over town to save 10 cents on an item." "How far apart can prices be from one supermarket to another?" "I shop for food where I do because they have lots of items that when you buy one you get one free." "I just like the place I shop at better." Certainly, there are valid reasons to prefer one business over another: it has fresher produce or seafood; it's the only one that carries that particular brand; it has more ethnic specialties or varieties; checkout is much quicker, and so on.

Good reasons, true; but unless you live in a remote rural area where that establishment is the only one of its kind around, it *does* pay to check prices in competing circulars and comparison-shop. It doesn't take that long to get a broad idea of prices for items you use or are interested in, and be able to select the place offering them at the best price. Most shopping usually involves standard items carried by almost any market in both major and "store" brands; they all carry the popular items that are boxed, bottled, canned, frozen, fresh, and packaged in cellophane or plastic. The real difference between places pretty much comes down to *prices,* and knowing how to shop creates competition, which helps control prices and can save you significant amounts of money. Permit me to share just a few real-life examples.

There's No Such Thing As A Free Lunch

Sometimes, a supermarket will offer a product with the added enticement of "Buy one at (price given), get a second of equal or lesser value free." Sounds good, but if you have any idea about a price range for that item, you'll know that it's no bargain; it's being offered to attract gullible shoppers. Typically, the price is more than doubled! For example, recently a supermarket offered USDA Choice top round London Broil at "Buy 1 at $4.99 per pound, get a second of equal or lesser value FREE!" That makes the true price about $2.50 a pound—not too bad, except that a nearby competitor priced the same product at $1.49 a pound.

Often, even within the same store, shoppers don't realize that an item they're looking for is on sale. They'll pick up a can of a well-known brand of sweet whole kernel golden corn selling for $1.09, and just two feet to the right is a competitive major brand of the same product on sale at "2 for 99 cents." I can't tell you how many shoppers I've seen pick up a popular brand of oven-stuffer roaster selling at $1.49 per pound, and in the same area is one from a major competitor on sale for 69 cents per pound. Once, three ladies each selected a two-pound bag of carrots for $1.69, when close to it was a five-pound bag on sale at $1.79! Such shoppers thank me when I point these things out to them.

Oh, yes, one more thing: Madison Avenue, take note—you can advertise the worth and value of almost any product, but when a competitive one is on sale in the stores, the shelves will be emptied before you can say, "What in hell did we do wrong?"

How To Get Gas

That gasoline prices vary among area stations is not unusual. Some sell major brands, others the so-called "off-brands." One or two may be located near shopping malls or right off a major highway. The resulting difference is usually only a few cents per gallon among the group—or was, until late June, 2006. By then, steadily increasing pump prices for the least expensive grade of gas had approached or topped three dollars a gallon in our area.

To visit the beautiful tri-states area that includes Port Jervis, New York, get off Route 84 at Exit 1 and, if you need to buy gas, there are five stations within a mile of each other. That June, their prices for regular gas (87 octane) ranged from $2.78 to $3.29 a gallon—a difference of 51 cents *per gallon*. O.K., so you're travelling; maybe you don't want to spend time hunting for gas stations, so you just pick one and fill up—fine. But the locals know; why aren't the expensive stations deserted? If an SUV (never mind an RV) takes even just 20 gallons, that's $10.20 you can save. Guess what? At 69 cents a pound, you just got a free 7½-lb. oven-stuffer roaster *and*, also for free, almost 3½ pounds of USDA top round London Broil at $1.49 a pound.

Don't Dismiss Food Coupons

Being divorced, efficient money management became critical, given the increased financial needs and undreamed-of expenses the situation created. There were many ways to save money, but using cents-off coupons to save a nickel here or a dime there (literally) surely could not be worth any serious consideration.

Or could it? What could possibly make me rethink coupons?

Y--- was coming over for the weekend and asked if there was anything we needed, since she was going grocery shopping after work on her way home anyway. The only thing that came to mind was espresso, since the amount on hand was barely enough to make one small pot. She said she'd get some and bring it with her when she came over the next day, which was Friday.

When she arrived after work, the kitchen table was instantly enhanced by a new temporary centerpiece in the form of a can of Medaglia D'Oro Espresso. I thanked her and asked how much it came to. She laughed and shook her head.

"Nothing," she responded.

"What do you mean, nothing? What, did you get it for free?"

Her eyes widened. "Better than that."

I was puzzled. "How could it be better than free?" Smiling, she then proceeded to explain.

She had a coupon offering $1 off the purchase price of any can of Medaglia D'Oro Espresso, and the supermarket at which she shopped offered "triple coupons"—that is, they would triple the value of any manufacturer's savings coupon—with no "up to 99 cents" limitation. At checkout, she gave her coupon to the lady, who began totaling all the groceries. When done, the lady tripled the coupon amount and deducted it from the total owed, so that $3 was saved on the espresso purchase. The can had a selling price of $2.89, so not only did Y--- get the espresso for free, but in the process she made a profit of 11 cents!

That one event made me rethink my ideas about careful food shopping; soon, savings coupons were being used.

I'm Not Proud: $5.70 Saved Is $10.00 Earned

Recently, while driving along Route 46 in New Jersey, I saw a supermarket and remembered that we needed three items for a fresh-vegetable salad. We parked in the lot, went inside, and found the three items, priced as follows:

- Sweet green peppers, $2.49 per pound
- Scallions (green onions), 99 cents per bunch
- Celery (it weighed 1½ pounds), $1.79 for one bunch.

Since I wanted to get several green peppers, three bunches of scallions and one bunch of celery, it would have cost:

- Four large green peppers (two-plus pounds), $5.10
- Three bunches of scallions, $2.97
- One celery (it weighed almost 1½ pounds), $1.79.

The three-item total would have run us $9.86.

Then I remembered that a few hundred feet up the road was an Asian food market. It turns out they had the needed items, but what a difference in prices:

- Sweet green peppers, 89 cents per pound (or $1.83 for slightly more than two pounds)
- Scallions, 48 cents per bunch (or $1.44 for 3 bunches)
- One celery (it weighed just over 2¼ pounds), 89 cents.

The same three-item total here came to $4.16—a savings of $5.70 on just three common food items! In addition to being less expensive, the produce offered at the Asian food market was fresher and more substantial: there were more scallions in each bunch, and the celery weighed about ¾ of a pound more.

If you're in the 40% tax bracket, you have to earn close to $10 to net $5.70. Better yet, if you're unemployed, retired or trying to make it on a fixed income, how significant does a gift or bonus like this "found" extra income become?

Chapter 4 –

Presidential Thoughts

How To Make Money Last

"If your organization contributed mucho bucks to my election campaign, there will be a number of profitable no-bid contracts awarded, from which you will make money.

"If your state's electoral votes were cast for me, your official requests for pork-barrel legislation will be carefully considered and approved, and all involved will make money.

"If you are an unquestioning member of my inner circle of cronies and relatives, an influential leader of a religious group whose beliefs parallel mine, an important lobbyist, a powerful union official, or a supportive international government leader, you will make money.

"If you're just a decent, honest, ethical American taxpayer not seeking any political favors or rewards but just trying to earn a living, be assured that if there's anything left, you will make money last."

"I Did Not Have Sexual Relations With That Woman"

That statement was made under oath by former Democratic President Bill Clinton during impeachment proceedings initiated during his second term by Christian Fundamentalists and other staunch Republican supporters, who attacked him with a level of vindictive passion that surpassed even the McCarthy hearings of the early 1950s.

The President had been the recipient of oral sex in the Oval Office of the White House, which they characterized as a public facility belonging to the American people. Asked if he had had sexual relations with the woman, his response was, "I did not have sexual relations with that woman." The Republicans were enraged, and accused him of lying. Well, guess what? He was actually telling the truth, and had those bumper-sticker believers had even one iota of experience or knowledge about sexual practices half a century earlier they would have understood that.

Decades ago, when I was a teenager, sexual accomplishments were described clearly and precisely, using baseball terms. For example, if a guy took his date to a drive-in movie, put his arm around her shoulder and was able to let his fingers hang down so that he could occasionally manipulate them to brush against her breast, and she didn't stop him, he got to "first base." A first kiss was in the same category, because we all knew that "if a girl can be kissed, she can be made." If, at some point, her blouse could be opened and the guy could "feel her up," or successfully discover the charms concealed under her skirt, he had gotten to "second base." To get to "third base," it was understood that there was "heavy petting," and that at least the guy had "come."

But unless he went "all the way" and "got laid," he did not "score." He had not had sex, and since that act of normal sexual intercourse was the only criterion for being able to brag that he had gone "all the way," nothing else counted as a "score." He could be gratified orally by a hundred females; he was still a virgin. Even an indulgence in anal sex could not change that. (Neither could any participation in same-sex or animal activities, although in those days such aberrations were virtually unknown and certainly never discussed.) The same was true for a gal: she could do whatever she wanted to sexually, but as long as her hymen was still intact, she was a virgin. She had not "put out," and therefore had not had sex with a man.

Did the President cheat on his wife and betray her trust? Yes. But did he have sex with that woman? No. Case closed.

The Transition From Clinton To Bush

In November of 2000, with President Clinton's second term nearly completed, it was time to elect a successor—something more easily said than done, as it turned out. In a surprising and controversial contest, the whole shebang came down to just one state: Florida; whoever won it would be

President in January. After weeks of problems, accusations and recounts, the U.S. Supreme Court chose George W. Bush as the winner.

It turned out to be a unique time in our nation's history: we went from the President-erect to the President-select.

National Elections? By Then, It's Too Late

Increasingly, fewer people are registering nationwide to vote or even bothering to go to the polls on an election day. Especially disturbing are the statistics for the 18- to 25-year-olds—the lowest of any group. Worse, these figures are mainly for major elections, such as for President or state Governor. Nobody even considers off-year or local elections, and that's what's truly frightening, because they are by far this nation's most important. How many crucial issues or races have been decided by fewer than five votes?

Tuesday, November 8, 2005 was Election Day in Orange County, New York State. It was barely mid-autumn, but recent unseasonably cold weather and an unexpected light snow shower almost overshadowed the significance of the day. Besides, it was an off year, and this election was just to vote for a few local judges and our local area's Legislator, just one of 21 representatives in the County's Legislature. He was seeking re-election and, as an incumbent with a good record of accomplishment with integrity in office, it was virtually a given that he would win, even though he was a Democrat in a heavily Republican county.

Well, he did win—by seven votes.

Of course, the losing opponent requested a recount, which was granted. While all military absentee ballots had been received well before the election and included in the original count, a few local-resident absentee ballots were late, even though they had been mailed and postmarked within the required time. It took ten days to do a complete recount, certify the results and announce the official winner. The results didn't change, except that now the incumbent's victory margin was 11 votes instead of seven.

11 votes! Out of the whole county, to win or lose by a lousy 11 votes! What if those three families down the road who never vote had decided to vote this time? They're devout Republicans, strict party-line adherents. Turns out some Democrats didn't vote, either. After all, in this County, the Republican candidates will all win anyway, except of course for our local Legislator, who will be re-elected hands down even if he is a Democrat, so why waste time and gas on something whose outcome is virtually assured? And who cares about party lines when it comes to court judges?

There were some other surprises throughout Orange County for both party candidates, and as a result the composition of the once heavily Republican-dominated Legislature was reshaped. Of its 21 seats, only 11 were still Republican; 10 were now controlled by Democrats. While Republicans still controlled the Legislature, it was by only one vote, which greatly increased the chances of one of them crossing party lines to support some bill introduced by Democrats that nevertheless would benefit the County as a whole.

And what about our local area's Democratic Legislator, who barely won re-election? As good as he may have been during his first term, he knows he'll have to work even harder this time, especially if he has hopes of someday representing more of his constituents in, say, the State Assembly or Senate. If that happens and goes well, who knows? We could use a good Congressman or Senator in Washington to fight for us, or a caring Governor to stay home and continue to address urgent needs and matters. Success at these levels would attract interest and attention on a national level, which might open new doors—even one, perhaps, at 1600 Pennsylvania Avenue...

If this seems like fantasizing or stretching things just a bit, let's remember that a person doesn't just wake up one morning, get out of bed, look thoughtfully out the window and announce, "Y'know, I think I'll run for President next November." And even if he or she does, we all know that's not the way the system works; even a "dark horse" candidate has to have started somewhere on the local level and advanced at least somewhat through the system.

This is why all of us have to become registered voters and exercise that privilege at election time. It's our only real chance to either give a promising candidate the opportunity to prove his or her worth and perhaps move on some day, or to put a quick end to the ambitions of an office-seeker whose abilities, qualifications or stand on issues leave you with negative feelings. Whether our choices win or lose the election, the total number of votes cast tells all candidates that we care and sends a very specific message to the winners: either stop playing the party politics game and work together for our benefit, or come the next election we'll be back—but you won't be.

Chapter 5 –

Time And Time Again, Relatively Speaking

Many expressions are prized because their basic truth and wisdom apply in everyday circumstances. The real gems, though, are those few that we recall when looking back over time at events or conditions, trying to put them into perspective. Perhaps the most significant of these is the powerful "Everything is relative."

This Time The Present Wins, Hands Down

As volunteer educators (I hate the term "docents") at our local canal museum, it had been a busy morning, with four of us leading eight classes of fourth graders on an informative guided tour that typically lasts about two and a half hours. June had just finished with her group, and I asked her how it had gone.

"Oh, all right, I guess," she responded, with a rueful smile. "I don't know, I guess I must be getting old."

"That's ridiculous," I countered. "What makes you say that?"

"Well," she said, perking up a bit, "I was telling the youngsters that if a canal boat wanted to turn around, it could do so in a clockwise or counterclockwise direction. I even made a forward, and then a reverse circular motion with my index finger. They just looked at me, then at each other. Their faces were totally blank, and I knew they had no idea what I was talking about. Many of them were wearing watches, so I said, 'Look at your watch; what do you see?' The answer I got was, 'Big numbers!' Every watch they had was digital, so not even one had a second hand that they could see going around. No wonder they didn't understand."

I knew how she felt; Barbara and I often use similar descriptive and once-familiar expressions which, sadly, are fast fading from the language as we approach the 21st Century. You're behind the wheel on a vacation trip, and you see something through the front windshield and announce, "Small plane coming in for a landing, eleven o'clock high." Every adult in that vehicle knows precisely where to look.

Barbara, in the passenger's seat, often points things out, and if she didn't pinpoint their location I'd miss them, since there's a limit to how long I can drive with my eyes off the road at 55 or 65 miles per hour. Once, she ecstatically exclaimed, "Oooh, cattle egrets in the field—two o'clock low." Happily, I got to see them.

But, that's progress. Someday, I guess, movie scenes depicting people using unfamiliar devices such as telephones with cords and dials will be as mystifying to some as the title of the 1949 movie "Twelve O'clock High" is now to others.

The Homes Of The Hollywood Stars

The lunch break came at a time that everyone in the publishing plant welcomed after a frenetic morning. The entire facility was working furiously as one unit to print the address labels needed to mail the November issue of several magazines to all subscribers throughout the nation. Put simply, the company's monthly cycle had arrived, and all were part of its period.

Louie, Harry and Walter gathered at their usual table in a back corner of the cafeteria, each with a lunchbox or paper bag. As was the custom, the consumption of sandwiches and other goodies was interspersed with detailed descriptions from Louie and Harry about the problems they had to deal with so far today, and how their respective solutions probably kept the company operating. There was a period of silence, then Louie announced that he was going bowling tonight and asked who wanted to come along.

Harry looked up. "Hey, that sounds good; what say, Walter?"

Walter gave him a sardonic smile. "Sure. Can you ask your brother if he'll go to college for me tonight?"

Harry grinned sheepishly. "Crap. I forgot about your damned classes." He paused for a few seconds, then spoke. "Sorry, but I gotta ask: you've been going to college at night for—what, three or four years now?" Walter nodded, then chimed in. "I started in September, '55; I'll have my B.S. degree in June of 1960.

"Yeah, great," Harry continued, "but why? And for what? Look, this is the way things are being done today. We got the best stuff: all the punch-card machines, verifiers, collators, sorters, printers…and they're all new Remington Rand! Throw in the Ampex tape drives down the other end and, jeez, we've got the top names in the field. Who's gonna threaten that? Plus you work here now, and have been; you know all these machines, and I know you like your job, and the company likes you. Hell, you've got it made."

"For now, yes," Walter countered, "but things can change, and if I need another job, college gives me an advantage. Besides, that degree may help me obtain a better job and earn more money."

Louie spoke up. "Hey, Walt, let me tell ya something. My old man had a car and bought a house right here in town, and he was married. He and my old lady raised me and Sal and Vinny, and he never earned more than ten grand a year."

"Well, that's terrific," Walter acknowledged, "but things aren't getting any cheaper. How much did that house cost him? Five or six thousand? Betcha it would sell for ten or twelve today. And what if I want a bigger home, in a different area? What if I'd like to have a summer home in the country, and two cars, maybe?"

"Oh, sure," Harry chimed in, "and I'd love to have a home like the Hollywood stars have. How much do they run?"

Walter thought for a second or two. "About a hundred grand or so, maybe 150. At least they did about five or ten years ago."

"There ya go," Harry concluded, triumphantly. "And you think you'll be able to live like that 'cause you went to college?" Louie nodded in agreement. "He's right, you know. No chance in hell."

Walter smiled and shrugged his shoulders. "Well, you've got a point, I guess. Still, it's nice to dream." He looked up, saw the clock. "Oops—almost time to head back. Take care, guys."

He stood up, collected his trash and dumped it on his way out. No sense trying to change anyone's mind. He remembered the old saying: *I'd rather lose an argument to a wise man than win one from a fool.* Those guys can live with their limited goals, but he knew that, with his degree, someday he'd earn more than $60 a week and be able to afford $100,000 for a mansion anywhere in the New York City area and certainly out in Beverly Hills.

Double Daylight Savings Time

As a youngster during the summer of 1945, near the end of World War II, I remember being in bed at ten o'clock at night and looking out the window. It was still light—not such that you could still be out there playing baseball, but enough to go for a walk down the road and see all the way to the bend with no need for a flashlight. As there was no moon, it had to be post-twilight dusk. And this was not the only such occurrence; every evening that summer featured a late light show.

Does anyone remember double daylight savings time? I've put that question to dozens of people over the years, but so far only three or four have known what I was referring to. How about you?

Respect Other People's Time

Sam had just finished a small project, one of several he'd been working on around the house as time permitted, and given his job schedule lately, free time had become a precious commodity, even on a Sunday. He looked at his watch; it was just after one-twenty. Hmmm…still almost 40 minutes before Len and Jo get here. Let's see, what else can be done? Well, there's that brush in the yard to be cleaned up. Nothing major, but he figures it will take a good half hour or so. That will leave less than 10 minutes to get out of his work clothes, shower, shave, get dressed and ready for them.

Nah, he decides, it'll be too close, especially if they get here a few minutes early; the yard work will just have to wait. Ellen, his wife, assures him that there's nothing he can do to help with any last-minute food preparation or table setup, so he does the get-ready bit and by ten minutes to two he is refreshed and waiting.

And waiting. And waiting…

It's 2:23; they're not here yet. This is just a bit more than being "socially late." Could they be lost? No; they've been here before. Traffic problems? Doubtful; not on these roads. Ellen, beginning to worry herself, urges him to stop grumbling and just be patient—they'll be here, she assures him. He nods but stays silent, keeping to himself the thought that has just popped into his mind: this isn't the first time they've been this late, or even the second.

He continues to wait. 2:30. Still no Len and Jo. Now he is a bit concerned. Many thoughts go through his mind. Something wrong at home? Car trouble, maybe? Unlikely; their Mazda is less than a year old. Besides, they've got a cell phone; in either case, they could call. But what if they got into an accident? He's really worried now.

At 2:36, their guests pull into the driveway. They both go out to meet them there, greeting them with some anxiety in their voices, telling them they were getting concerned, and asking if everything's all right. "Oh, yeah," Len replies, "we just got started a little late. Had a few things to take care of—y'know."

The fingers of her hand around Sam's arm tighten and loosen in four urgent cycles. He understands the veiled message and, since experience has taught him that in such matters his wonderful Ellen is always right, he closes his mouth, lets it expand into a forced smile and totally changes his reply.

"Hey," he tells them, "as long as everything's all right, that's all that matters. Good to see you again; come on in and relax."

It's an enjoyable afternoon and evening, with a superb dinner, and when they leave around 8:30 warm goodbyes are exchanged. "We *must* get together again soon," Jo gushes, then pauses. "Uh, let me think…the rest of this month and part of next month are shot…maybe October. Yeah, I'll call you guys in mid-October."

"Sounds good," Sam's sweetie assures her. "Meanwhile, travel well and get home safely." They get into their car and back out onto the road, honking to acknowledge their waving hosts, and begin their trip home. Sam and Ellen head inside for the night.

"Thank you for not saying anything," Ellen said, smiling. "I know they've done this before, and you certainly had every right to be angry, but you were smart to keep it all to yourself."

Sam looked at her. "I was thinking about last week, when that guy from Sears said he'd be here in the morning, and you had to wait here for him all day because he didn't show up until 3:30." He paused. "Honey, what pisses me is that I could have cleaned up all that brush and gotten it into the mulch pile. I didn't need more than 30, maybe 40 minutes. Now it'll have to wait 'til next week, when I could have painted the guest bathroom and given it two coats. Damn! That really pisses me off! Don't they ever think about anyone else's time but their own? Not to even mention our worries. Are they all right? Maybe they hit a deer."

There was silence for a few seconds, then he continued. "I'll tell you this, though, baby: the next time we set up to have them here I'm telling them that we would really appreciate it if they got here on time or close to it, and if they ask what the problem is, I'll tell them in a nice way. And whenever they're scheduled to be here, whatever time that is, I'll be outside doing stuff. If they get here on time, give or take ten minutes, fine; I'll stop. But more than that, and I continue for a good half hour or so after they do arrive and if they don't like it, tough crap. I don't think we've *ever* done anything like that to anyone, *ever*. In fact, think of Tommy and Karen, when we go down to New Jersey to see them. He knows we've got a hundred-mile trip each way, but you know as well as I do that if we're more than a few minutes late, he's ready to call every hospital in the area. Right?"

"Yes, dear," she responded, quietly.

"Good. Then that's what I'll do next time they come up here. Maybe it'll teach those thoughtless morons to have some respect for other people's time. And if that offends them, we don't have to have them up here again—assuming they still want to know us."

"Yes, dear," she repeated, sighing patiently. Ellen knew he'd calm down, but she also knew Sam. Len and Jo were nice people, but like too many, their primary concern was themselves and their wants. Sam had turned the other cheek more than once. He valued friendships, but that should be a two-way street. There was a limit to giving people the benefit of the doubt and being forgiving, and that limit had been reached.

Three strikes and you're out.

Maybelline's Confirmation

Driving along historic Alamo Parkway was usually a pleasure, since it was one of northern Florida's most beautiful roads. Not this time, though; the rain had begun to fall. Bentley was furious.

"What in hell is this? Look at this sloshy crap! Didn't the goddamned Weather Bureau predict a warm, sunny day? Screwed up again."

"Honey, relax," Tiffany urged, turning her head towards the driver's side. "You know they've been wrong more than they've been right since the '23 Storm Cycle."

Bentley grimaced. Who could forget 2023? God's wrath had graced Florida with its worst storms in 30 years and, surprisingly, most of them had devastated the area north of Orlando. "Yeah, I know, but couldn't they have been right just this once, with this confirmation to go to? Those storms were last year."

"Everything'll be OK," she promised, soothingly. "Everyone'll get to the church in time and be able to park and get inside without drowning, you'll see. Boy, you're really grouchy today—had a bad night's sleep, I'll bet."

"Yeah, I guess so," Bentley grunted, "but we're lucky. We're only a few blocks away, I think. Where do we turn?"

Tiffany didn't even have to look at the directions that had come with the invitation. She knew them, having read them and just about memorized them earlier this morning. "Toyundai Street."

A minute or so later, he spotted the street sign and turned right onto Toyundai. The rain had just about let up; in fact, the sky was getting brighter as the sun struggled to shine its way through the thin cloud veil. Two, three, four blocks—suddenly, Tiffany called out, "There! On your left—at the corner of Verizon." Awed, she paused a couple of seconds, then whispered, "Wow! Look at it!"

They had arrived at St. Peterbilt's Church of the Ever-Vigilant

Fundamentalists, the most original but controversial building in Daytona Beach. Pausing at the intersection, Bentley studied the three-story blue concrete structure, with its gleaming glass and aluminum highlights. It had been deliberately angled to face the intersection in such a way that only the front of the building could be fully observed. Halfway up there was a slight crease, causing the upper half of the church to recede in such a way that the tinted glass comprising the upper third of the front faced skyward. At the left front corner there was a rectangular window of diaphanous glass at the first-floor level, symmetrically replicated on the right. Between these windows was a tall, impressive pair of doors with a façade of vertical chromium strips, every other one painted glossy black. From the bottom of the doors to the patterned bluestone on the ground, the riser connecting them became part of the bold steel strip that ran across the entire front of the building.

Turning left, Bentley cruised for a few feet, then turned right into the church parking lot. Happily, the rain had stopped; he and Tiffany exited the car without umbrellas and began walking slowly towards the front doors. As they did, a thought struck him.

"Say, honey, isn't Aurora a Reawakened Conservationist?"

"Conservative, you dufus, not conservationist," she responded, giggling. "Yes, she is, which is why she belongs to the FedEx Church of Deliverance."

He frowned. "Then tell me, why didn't she have Maybelline's confirmation at her own church? Doesn't that make sense?"

"Remember, her own church is not that big. I don't think it can hold more than two, two hundred fifty people. Besides, this place looks much more elegant and—well, you know, it's classy, glamorous." Reaching the entrance, they stepped inside.

The entrance area was typically small, with racks along the far wall. They held the usual religious brochures and pamphlets—descriptive, question-and-answer, prayers and hymns appropriate for this calendar day—along with membership applications and a large, beautifully carved Honduran mahogany box for donations. Between the last rack and the entrance into the nave stood a large narrow table, laden with carefully arranged product samples and coupons that reinforced the gospel of the advertising posters along the walls, set below the fading photographs of bygone ministers.

Bentley, once a Catholic, was surprised to see what appeared to be a holy water font just to his left. Above it, on the wall, was a small poster that proclaimed, "At Least Be Pure Within Yourself." Within the font, thoughtfully, were bottles of Poland Spring water.

He and Tiffany entered the nave, which resembled the stadium-like facilities used by televangelists but was less than half the size. Pausing momentarily, Tiffany looked towards the audience seating in the front, just before the altar. As she suspected, that area was reserved today for the young communion participants, who would be welcomed into the church as a group. Taking Bentley's arm, they made their way to the group and, having spotted Maybelline in the very first row, walked over to her, greeted her warmly and offered her their congratulations. Just to the left were her proud parents, who were smiling at them. Tiffany and Bentley repeated their greetings and sincere congratulations, then continued their walk towards the north transept. It was time to sit down.

Bentley wanted to sit way at the back for a quick exit once the show was over, so they selected two aisle seats just four rows from the entrance doors. As they sat, the minister stood up and began walking across the sanctuary towards the altar. Good timing.

The cushioned benches were actually comfortable, and Bentley really started to relax. Scanning the nave from the advantageous perspective of his rear bench seat, he could really appreciate its size and tasteful décor. He was especially admiring of the stained glass windows, each of which held an exquisite representation of the product most closely associated with the sponsoring corporation. Surrounding the product, of course, were the usual cherubs or shepherds. His favorite was the one of the minister in his surplice, topped by a cassock and a stole. On the cassock, between the sides of the stole, was an unobtrusive black check mark. It was just large enough for the worshipper looking at it to recognize it and know that this was a Nike window. Talk about classy, good taste. What puzzled him, however, were the televisions, one on each wall of the north and south transepts just in front of the sanctuary. Both were the old, outdated 84-inch models that were far too small to project images clearly to those seated where he was or way up front, off to the sides.

Staring at the leftmost set, Bentley's eyes were getting heavy and, given the rotten night's sleep he'd had, he didn't fight it.

What finally woke him up was Tiffany's gentle but persistent nudging. Everyone was starting to leave; it was all over. He had missed the confirmation, but since it was performed as a group event, he would probably not have been able to see Maybelline specifically anyway, so he felt he didn't miss that much. Besides, he was feeling a little more alert, and was totally in favor of being ahead of the exiting crowd and getting to the parking lot quickly.

It was good to be heading home. If traffic remained this light, they could cover the forty miles in less than two hours. He'd still have time to give the bookcase he had built one last coat of walnut stain; next weekend he'd finish the project with a coat of varnish.

He turned the radio on right in the middle of a commercial for Trojans. *Damn,* he thought, irritated that he had missed the first part. It was his favorite ad—the one with the London Symphony Orchestra and the Vienna Boys Choir. He sang along. At the end, an exuberant announcer invited each listener to guess the number of commercials that the station had aired during the past hour and phone in the answer. If you were the ninth caller and were correct, you would win $1,000 in cash. Bentley didn't know the number, of course, but he realized how easy it was to figure it out. Given no more than three minutes of music, followed by at least three minutes of 30-second spots *(let's see, that's six ads in six minutes, so that's 60 in 60 minutes)*, the answer probably was 60. He was half tempted to call in his answer, but he knew that by the time he recited the station's number to the dashboard calling system and it forwarded it, the ninth caller probably would have gotten through.

Reaching McDonald's Interstate 95, he selected the southbound entrance and continued his trip home.

Whatever Happened To Rap?

Joe finished preparing his snack and left the kitchen to return to the entertainment room for the final round of the World Cleavage Competition from Brussels. *This has to end in half an hour,* he thought, remembering that the same World Sports Network was supposed to televise the full European Women's Wet Underarm Hair Contest from Paris at 4:00 o'clock.

Passing his son's bedroom, he heard a strange combination of noises that stopped him in his tracks. What kind of soda pop was that kid drinking that produced those kinds of belches? Worse yet, other gas-emission sounds were included, along with pig-snorts. Still, Joe could not help but admire how skillfully they were all interbesprinkled throughout the random banging of a tom-tom.

"Son, *what* is going on here?"

Dave looked up, startled at the interruption, but with eyes wide open and lustrous, his head bobbing up and down knowingly.

"Dad, that's Schoko Schnitten! It's his latest hit, *'Gain Us an Anus.'* Are you saying you haven't even heard it? It's Number One worldwide! Wow! And I thought you liked German music."

Joe started to respond, but Dave suddenly held up his hand and began waving it energetically, along with his head, from side to side. "Wait, wait— here comes the end. Dad! Catch this!"

Joe listened as the asynchronous sounds rose to a crescendo, then stopped suddenly. A second later, the tom-tom began beating furiously for a few seconds and stopped, at which point a male voice screamed, "Fuck my sheep!" After a breathtaking silence, the bleating of a sheep was heard for about a minute, after which the recording engineer mercifully ended the number in the usual creative manner—with a 30-second fadeout.

Dave, his voice trembling with excitement, looked hopefully at his father. "Well? What did you think? Come on, dad—you *had* to like it! It's so succulent!"

Joe smiled. "It's not bad, but I wouldn't download it. I guess I just don't like today's—what you kids call music. Hey, enjoy, but remember you got homework, and there's school tomorrow." Turning, Joe and his snack resumed the walk to the entertainment room.

Ellen looked up and smiled as he entered. "What were you two listening to? It sure sounded awful."

"God, the crap these kids listen to today—geez. Boy, I'll tell you one thing: the days of good stuff are gone. Do you remember rap? Do you think he's ever even heard *one* rap piece? Hell, you can't even download that stuff; even Oldtime doesn't offer it anymore."

Helen's smile became wistful. "Joe, you can't live in the past. It's 2040, not 2010; this is Dave's time and his music, not yours." She paused momentarily, then set down her sewing and stood up. "Well, anyway, if you'll excuse me, I have to finish preparing dinner. Don't snack too much."

"Well, still," he grumbled, sitting down and carefully balancing the snack in his lap. He stared at the set. The competition was highlighting a Liechtenstein beauty whose cleavage was to drool for, but Joe's mind had drifted well beyond Brussels to a bedroom in which a teenager was listening to a compact disc. He closed his eyes to better concentrate, then smiled as he both saw himself and heard the selection in his mind more clearly. It was *"Restless,"* as performed by Sha'piquewa La Cha'toomba. It had been the best-selling rap single in 2010 and even now, 30 years later, Joe could still hear the percussion *(boomboom baah, b'boomboom b'baah, boomboom baah, b'boomboom b'baah)* and totally recall the lyrics exactly as they had been rhythmically recited:

I didn't want to sit, 'cause I hadda take a shit,
But my girlfriend had a fit, so I punched her in the tit.
Then she grabbed my hand and bit, so I kicked her in the clit.
Now she shows that she has grit, as she digs into her kit,
Almost tearing off her mitt, and pulls out a can of Flit.
She is really in a snit, as she sprays and hits my zit.
Now I'm angry at this chit, who is acting like a twit.
She must really be half lit, 'cause she don't know when to quit.
When I tell her she should git, she asks, "Why? I'm lovin' it!"
And goes right on with the skit, even calling me a nit.
(She must think that she's a Brit, 'cept she doesn't have the wit.)
So I hold her face and spit; now she knows it's time to split.

Joe's eyes moistened and a wave of nostalgia flowed gently through his chest, warming his heart. As his focus returned to the television set, he realized how lucky he was. The crap kids listen to today? You can have it. Rap—now *there* was a class act.

Chapter 6 –

Attitude With Latitude

So Europeans Are Multi-Lingual: Big Deal

Americans have always admired (and perhaps even envied) people who are fluent in more than one language and can switch from one to another in the blink of an eye. We've all seen it happen: perhaps you're talking to someone and her cell phone rings. She apologizes to you, answers it, her face lights up and suddenly her speech becomes totally unintelligible to you. Or you might be in a small store, talking to someone behind the counter, when one of the staff comes out and tells him something in a foreign language to which he responds effortlessly.

Generations ago our families had that same ability—after all, everyone came to this country from somewhere overseas, where the language spoken was something other than English (except for the hundreds of thousands of New Englanders who somehow all managed to come over on the *Mayflower*). For the most part, however, that multi-linguistic ability has disappeared among native-born Americans over subsequent generations. In fact, we're almost embarrassed to admit that all we can speak is English. Europeans in particular are especially adroit at making us feel guilty about being linguistically challenged, since many of them speak two, three, even five languages, of which English is one.

Big goddamned deal! Of course they speak more than one language—it's Europe, for God's sake! If our nation was made up of 50 separate countries instead of 50 united states, we too would all speak more than one language.

Living where I do, of course I'd speak New Yorkese; I would probably also be fluent in Pennsylvaniash and Jerseyish, with some ability to get along in Connecticutese and Delawarean. I might even know words or a few idiomatic expressions in Vermontese or New Hampshirish. And if any European country was as comparably influential or important in world affairs as ours is, I'm sure we'd all be required to take its language as a course in school and learn it fluently.

As we may have to do in the near future with Chinese, Arabic or some dialect of Indian.

She's A Single Mom

Is she a woman with a couple of children, divorced from her philandering or abusive husband and trying her best to make ends meet by working two minimum-wage jobs with no help from her deadbeat ex? Or is she a 15-year-old ninth-grade bottom-of-her-class slut who seduced some cool dude, got knocked up, had to drop out and is now receiving government welfare funds and food stamps while shacking up with yet another pimply-faced loser?

Physician, Heal Thyself

There are doctors who will not perform an abortion because it violates their religious beliefs, even if the victim's assailant was a family member. Similarly, there are faith-based public hospitals that will not administer a morning-after pill to a rape victim, even if she requests it and is there not by choice but because it's the only facility around. Likewise, there are pharmacists who will not sell condoms or fill prescriptions for birth-control devices. That these professionals have morals or ethical standards is fine, but nobody forced them into their line of work; they freely chose to help people who depend on them. If these issues cause such personal problems and anguish, then they should get the hell out of their professions and get a job on an assembly line producing "Jesus Loves You" bumper stickers or religious figures for vehicle dashboards and rear-view mirrors.

Isn't God Supposed To Be A Positive Force?

The evening news highlights the capture of a man who held up a liquor store, smashed the windows of a pharmacy across the street and escaped in a stolen car. When captured, he fully admitted his guilt, but when asked why he did these things his response was, "God spoke to me and told me to do it."

There are many such incidents nationwide every year. What I want to know is, how come when my doorbell rings and I answer it, there's never a man standing there proclaiming, "God spoke to me and told me to mow your lawn this summer and shovel your driveway this winter."?

Save Our Forests

Conservationists, environmentalists, scientists and nature lovers have authored a plethora of books stressing how critical it is for the future of humanity that we preserve our forests and woodlands. Collectively, millions of copies of these books have been printed.

How many trees has *that* cost our forests?

Don't Be Transfused About The Red Cross

The American Red Cross began as an organization with noble objectives and purposes that operated for decades in a caring way unlike any other, ever, anywhere. But somewhere along the way, something happened and, sadly, all that changed.

The worst floods in half a century hit the northeast during the summer of 1955. The area around Stroudsburg, Pennsylvania and parts of southeastern Connecticut were especially hard hit, but perhaps worst of all was Port Jervis, New York, the point at which the combined Neversink River and Basha Kill join the Delaware River. The bridge that crosses the Delaware between Port Jervis and Matamoras, Pennsylvania remained closed for a couple of days until the water level dropped below the bridge's grated span. Pike Street, the road in Port that takes you to the bridge, was closed because its 12-foot, 6-inch-deep underpass was totally submerged. Nearby, some multi-storied light-colored buildings had a stain line running between the first and second stories that brought to mind "ring around the bathtub." Not surprisingly, ground-level stores and shops were inundated. Fortunately, the city's own fire and police departments, as well as other local and surrounding organizations, were quick to respond, helping with rescue and cleanup operations, shipments and distribution of food and supplies, traffic and security control and so much more.

Spending summers in the area surrounding Port Jervis, we were trying to help in those parts that, too, had been flooded. It was a day or so before we could even get into Port but when we did, the progress made by the restoration efforts was noticeable. A group of residents we knew spoke quietly about the damage but were appreciative of the help, especially from The Salvation Army.

"What about the Red Cross?" my father inquired of one.

Some looked at each other with raised eyebrows or shook their heads or smirked or smiled, but the collective message was clear.

"Oh yeah, they were here, all right—selling coffee. Right over there," he responded, pointing to a specific location. A few of the others nodded in agreement.

It was amusing, except he wasn't joking, and further discussion only verified his statement. I was surprised—even disappointed—but when I told this story to others, some recounted their own Red Cross experiences. Included were more coffee-selling opportunities and other financially creative operations. For example, a few who had served in the Armed Forces overseas during World War II remembered cartons of cigarettes arriving from U.S. tobacco companies that were intended to be handed out to the troops but were instead being sold to them by the Red Cross.

These unsavory practices might not have been universal within the Red Cross, and I suppose it is possible that those who shared their stories might have misinterpreted or misunderstood what they saw. But with so many similar recollections from so many people from various war zones, something had to be wrong; after all, of all organizations, why choose to lambaste the Red Cross?

Since then, a cycle seems to have developed that gives credence to these earlier stories. Things would be quiet for awhile, then the Red Cross would initiate one of its periodic appeals to the public for financial contributions and blood donations. Then something would happen to involve them in a negative way. It might be a "late" response to a natural disaster, or an inefficient distribution of relief supplies and funds, or an inexplicable shortage of blood following a highly successful drive just preceding the disaster, or an internal financial scandal. It would be reported, but the public brushed it aside. After all, this was the Red Cross; there must be some valid reason for it. In time, the problem faded away and was forgotten by the masses.

Things would be quiet for awhile, then the Red Cross would initiate one of its periodic appeals to the public for financial contributions and blood donations...

Plaintiff And Lawyer And Judge—Oh, My!

What has happened to our so-called legal system? The number of asinine lawsuits making it to court, or lawyers willing to take on such cases, is growing. Some jury decisions or awards are totally inexplicable, yet few judges will throw out such cases or reverse a jury's verdict. Here are just a few recent examples, some of which you may remember.

In Brooklyn, New York, some teenager decided to break in and rob a local public school. He selected a dark night and got to the school, only to discover that each window had bars across it. Undeterred, he somehow managed to scale the building and climb up onto the roof. Peering around, he spotted a door behind which he figured were stairs that could get him down to the classrooms, if it wasn't locked. He began walking across the roof towards the door when he tripped over an unseen skylight, smashed through the glass and fell to the floor, injuring himself. He was apprehended but sued the school for damages, claiming that his injuries, pain and suffering was their fault because it was their skylight.

Guess what? You're right—*he won the case!*

An 82-or-so-year-old woman drove up to the takeout window at a McDonald's and gave in her order, which included a cup of coffee. When the order was filled, she took the coffee cup and set it between her legs and started to drive. As the car pulled away from the window some of the hot coffee spilled on her legs, causing the woman to suffer some bad painful burns. She sued McDonald's, claiming that her burns were caused by their having made such hot coffee and, incidentally, serving it in a cup that had no "Caution: Hot Liquid" warning on it.

Guess what? Yup, you're right again—she not only won her case but was also awarded something like 3.2 *million* dollars!

(McDonald's appealed the verdict; it was overturned, and a far more reasonable settlement was reached. But the fact that the old lady's carelessness or stupidity was rewarded so lavishly in the first place was a source of concern and disbelief to all.)

Here's another example involving a fast-food chain. Some fellow sued his local Burger King because their foods had increased both his weight and "bad" cholesterol to dangerous levels. He dined there almost exclusively because the selections were so varied, tempting and delicious that they were irresistible to him. Besides, he noted, there were no signs anywhere warning customers about what these foods could do to their health or weight, nor was anything posted listing any item's ingredients and corresponding amounts of fats, cholesterol, sodium or other potentially harmful ingredients. And get this: in several interviews, he stated with completely credible sincerity that *he had no idea that cheese-topped burgers, shakes, French fries or other such fast foods might cause weight or health problems,* and since Burger King didn't alert or warn him of any risks or dangers, it was their fault, not his.

(Fortunately, after hearing the basics of this ridiculous case the judge threw it out of court, telling the plaintiff that since Burger King was virtually the only place at which he ate, he could have figured out what was making him fat and causing his health problems. But still, the case made it to court.)

Many food and drink establishments feature a "karaoke night," where anyone can get up in front of an audience and perform—that is, sing along with a song being played on a piano. The words are projected onto a large screen behind the singer, who is also shown. Recently, though, some places have changed to "platform dancing" to allow customers to get up and gyrate rather than sing.

Apparently, a zealous 22-year-old performer got carried away one evening and migrated from the floor to the top of a piano, where she continued to dance until she lost her footing and fell, hitting the floor and injuring herself. She's in the process of suing the place, claiming (of course!) that they're responsible because the piano that caused her to fall is theirs. The case is going to court.

Are you ready for this? In 2007 a Washington, D.C. judge sued his dry cleaner for $65 million dollars because *they lost his pants!!* But wait—there's more, and I swear, I'm not making this up: In June or July of the same year *the case actually went to trial!*

Perhaps this is why the system is costly and so backed up that it could be months or even years before a case gets to court. Maybe what is needed is for a judge to refuse to hear such cases or, better yet, warn a plaintiff's lawyer that if he wastes the court's time with another case like this he'll be heavily fined and/or have his license suspended for six months. And if any judge is unwilling to try or at least consider this approach, maybe he or she should be removed from the bench for awhile.

O, Nostradumus: Didn't You Forget Something?

The famed 16th-century doctor-turned-predictor is credited with forecasting many significant events over the next four hundred-or-so years.

His skilled but cryptic style of writing allowed his references to be interpreted loosely and applied broadly to events worldwide. His admirers and followers insisted that not only had he predicted many major events accurately but had even foreseen and described comparatively smaller occurrences, such as specific World War II battles. He was also credited with many varied predictions, including one in which he envisioned a better world for all whose lives were spent in ceaseless backbreaking physical toil.

What's amazing, though, is that a man who could miraculously foresee a single battle confrontation and allude to a better physical world for humanity never foresaw or even hinted at something as obvious, omnipresent and mentally earthshaking as the computer.

Got Milk Money?

Sometime in the late 1990s the dairy industry (to use a general term) began a clever campaign to increase milk sales. A series of ads began to appear in many varied publications that featured one or more well-known recognizable sport or entertainment personalities. One ad might use a football hero, another the stars from a television soap opera and, after that, perhaps two well-known tennis legends who just happened to be sisters. Every one, though, had the same theme: each celebrity, sporting a milk moustache, would look right at you and ask, "Got Milk?" The series has been successful enough that it's still running, almost a decade later.

Strangely, though, something happened almost as soon as the ads began running. As hard as it is to believe, the price of milk began to increase—significantly, noticeably and steadily. It wasn't that long before the price of a gallon of milk had almost doubled in some areas of the nation (from around $1.79 to over $3.49 a gallon). What could have caused this to happen? Could the slightly remote possibility that these noble bastions of entertainment were being compensated or rewarded for their labors be a contributing factor?

I tried, but my efforts to find answers failed quickly. Every ad is copyrighted by "America's Milk Processors"; none ever provided a real company name, much less a fax or telephone number or web address, so there was no one to contact. People with knowledge of advertising agencies and public relations firms had no idea who was behind the campaign; on-line research yielded nothing. Meanwhile, the usual familiar Mother Nature excuses were being resurrected: we'd had an unusually cold and snowy winter, a late spring, a long hot dry summer, a wet chilly autumn with an early frost, and so on.

In almost ten years, prices still have not come down. Worse yet, as with so many other agricultural products, everyone continues to benefit from retail price increases except the farmers who supply the goods and we foolish customers who continue to purchase them.

How To Speed Up Telephone Customer Service

With rare exception, we all know that it's virtually impossible to call a company and get through to a customer service person. Even if you can navigate your way through the menu selections and find one that actually meets your needs or finally tells you what key to press to speak to a human being, chances are you'll be eligible for Social Security by the time your call is attended to. And whether you have a problem or just want to ask a simple question, it doesn't matter—you're going to have to wait.

Unless you select the menu option that is offered if you wish to purchase one of the company's products or subscribe to one of its services. Press that button and you can almost guarantee that you'll be conversing with a live, cheerful, accommodating person within 763 nanoseconds.

Exposing Pork, Poultry And Ponies

Never having tried Campbell's Pork and Beans (it sounded like such an enticing combination), I once bought a can out of curiosity, opened it and emptied the contents onto a plate. All I could see were syrupy-looking beans punctuated by occasional pieces of what appeared to be blobs of white fat. *Where's the pork*, I wondered. The next day I asked some co-workers what that stuff was and was assured, "that's the pork!" Were they serious? My God, I've seen congressional legislation that contains more pork. I was reminded of the Spanish dish "arroz con pollo," which translates to "rice with chicken" but is more familiarly known in the U.S. as "chicken with rice." Why? Although I've enjoyed the dish both homemade and in restaurants, it's always presented with noticeably more rice than chicken (unlike its French counterpart "poulet au riz").

Why not call it what it is? To me, that's like creating a dish comprised of "equal parts of rabbit and horsemeat"—that is, one rabbit to one horse—and calling it "rabbit stew."

Class Versus Crass

You can tell a lot about people just by the way they order food in a restaurant and the tone of voice they use. Let's eavesdrop on the duo at that table, where the waiter has just arrived and asked one of them, "May I take your order?"

The first one begins, pleasantly. "Yes, thank you. I'd like to start with a salad, please, and could I please have it with the house dressing on the side? Oh, and for a soup, the chicken noodle sounds good; may I have just a cup? Then, I think the lasagna would be lovely; I'd like to try that. And could I please have some iced tea? Thank you."

The waiter finishes writing and turns to the second diner with a smile. "And may I take your order?" The other begins, brusquely. "Yes, I'll have a salad; give me some ranch dressing on the side, in a separate container—I don't want it on the salad—and I want a cup of vegetable soup. Then I'm going to have the baked chicken, and, uh, bring me an iced tea."

If you had to, which one would you rather get to know better?

Pin The Tail On The Public

Each state has several representatives, two United States senators to represent its people in Washington, D.C., and a governor. All of these officials are elected by residents of that state. Sometimes, depending on the public appeal of a given Presidential candidate in a national election, all winning candidates can be from that party. In an off-year election, however, the public can voice its disappointment with Washington politics and vote for congressional candidates from a different party. This can create a more balanced Congress in Washington; it can even change which party controls the Senate and/or the House of Representatives.

But sometimes a Senator is unable to complete the six-year term. Lately there have been a few such instances caused by resignations (scandals), illnesses (a stroke, for one) and even death (a plane crash, for another). In such cases that state's Governor appoints a replacement—an apparently practical solution, except for one minor point: there is nothing to prevent the Governor from selecting a member of his or her own party and, typically, that's what happens.

This is outrageous. If that state's voters elected, say, a Democrat to represent them in the Senate, then a replacement should be from that same party. The fact that the Governor is a Republican (or, for that matter, a member of any other political party) should not give him or her the right to override the public's choice. This practice to me is as infuriating as politically motivated gerrymandering. Both should be clarified and standardized by fair definitive legislation.

It's Always The One Per Cent

Most people just want to be left alone to pursue their everyday activities in peace and get some pleasure and enjoyment out of life while doing so. They're good folk who have been taught to practice the basic decencies implicit in the Golden Rule, universal to all nationalities and which, for the most part, works. It encourages recognition of shared good qualities yet respects any idiosyncratic differences. Such tolerance can resolve or perhaps even prevent large-scale problems. Most of us have friends, family members or significant others of different faiths, but if they're good people to whom we're committed, who can say that their views (or lack thereof) of God are wrong or that ours are more acceptably correct?

They can; that minority of misfits anywhere, at any time, that purport to speak for God. Power-crazed or disillusioned, they have the uncanny ability to appeal to others with pent-up frustrations over unrealized dreams that need a scapegoat. Typically, these "others" are at the bottom of the educational scale, receptive to a redeemer who assures them that it's not their fault that they're failures; God loves them, so it's got to be someone else, some other group that interprets God's word differently, hence incorrectly. Unfortunately, one can't argue definitively against such dubitable issues, and soon our lives are affected—even endangered—by these verbal viruses.

Here is just one common example. The population explosion (or perhaps "copulation explosion" is a more accurate term) that has become a worldwide problem is due, in part, to the unwillingness of some faiths to allow birth control to be taught or practiced because it conflicts with their perception of God's word and is sinful. God, after all, said, "Be fruitful and multiply." Actually, the expression translates more accurately to "Be fertile and reproduce," which is quite different and would permit, shall we say, litter control. But even if they're right, if they so believe in God, when do they stop assuming His role and trust Him to deliver justice to those "sinners" indulging in contraception? Or isn't their faith that strong?

On a lighter note, even personal adherence to a religious belief can be reconsidered, with benefits. Case in point: many people are vegetarians not for health reasons but because they believe that, in the Sixth Commandment, God commanded, "Thou shalt not kill." Actually, what He said translates more to "Thou shalt not murder."

Some Comic Strips Are No Laughing Matter

Opinionated commentary on various matters of public interest has always been an important part of newspapers and magazines, and one of the most effective ways to make a point has been through the use of cartoons and comic strips. One can only imagine the challenge of humorously describing a situation or presenting a viewpoint in one or even a few creatively-captioned drawings using satire and allegory in ways that can still be appreciated and understood, even if not accepted, by readers of any persuasion.

But what's disturbing, even ominous, is when other tactics are used to make a point. Alarms sound when clever depiction of an issue for consideration by people of flexible intelligence is replaced by blatant, vicious propaganda intended only to strengthen the arguments of the rigidly opinionated.

Two left-leaning political comic strips, *"Doonesbury"* and *"Non Sequitur,"* are more than matched by the unarguably right-wing *"Mallard Fillmore."* The first two adhere to the custom of voicing opinions satirically or allegorically, with veiled subtlety and humor, somewhat in the manner of *"Aesop's Fables."* Whether one agrees or disagrees with the viewpoints, at least they necessitate thought, especially when critical of either side of an issue. By contrast, with rare exception, *"Mallard Fillmore"* doesn't even pretend to bother with such a mentally burdensome effort. It becomes nothing more than a vitriolic diatribe against anything in defiance of ultra-conservative or fundamentalist views of righteous living. When our nation, at peace, prospered under Democratic President Bill Clinton, somehow, miraculously, only "family-values"-oriented Republicans caused such good to happen. Anything negative, of course, was Clinton's fault, especially after the Oval Office incident (which Republicans turned into a costly but opportune scandal). *"Mallard Fillmore"* was at its peak and unrelenting in its one-sided attacks.

Then George W. Bush succeeded Clinton and became, perhaps, the worst President in American history; *"Mallard Fillmore"* never even alluded to the arrogant Texan. As the Bush-created global catastrophes increased in intensity and number, the strip simply diverted attention from them by blaming critics of his policies for causing these woes and contributing to the moral decline of "family values." It alluded to the ACLU, Hollywood, gays, Ivy League schools, *"The New York Times,"* schoolteachers, free-speech or pro-choice advocates, defenders of same-sex civil unions, stem-cell research, doctor-assisted suicides, birth control—anything but Bush or his inner circle of suck-ups. There even were times when things were so disastrous that the strip simply ignored them and resorted to painting historical "leftists" as a hindrance to "progress" then and the probable cause of similar problems today!

One can criticize the strip among friends and elicit opinions, but the result of any such discussion is predictable. Regardless of topic, those whose political inclinations lean towards the right will counter with "Well, '*Doonesbury*' does the same thing" or, worse yet, give an unrelated Fox News Channel-inspired analogy. ("Some industry operations are causing dangerously high decibel levels in parts of the country." "So, what has that got to do with industry? I was listening to the radio yesterday, and Barbara Streisand was singing pretty loud.") Just as bad is the uncaring indifference of those on the left, who usually respond with "Oh, I don't read 'Fillmore'."

What's concerns me is that I've yet to hear or read any public criticism of *"Mallard Fillmore."* Not being an extremist on either side I believe in "free speech," but that privilege has societal limits (since words like "slander" and "libel" do exist), and if no outcry or protest is forthcoming, the next level of abuse will be attempted. Just as children test the limits of acceptable behavior and must be supervised or disciplined to enforce them, the same principles must be applied to adult activities. Otherwise, we risk becoming another 1930s Germany, which used simple, amusing drawings of hook-nosed Zionists, liberals in the arts and loathsome gays to direct blame for its problems and, when unchallenged, quickly increased its repressive actions and set the next level of acceptable behavior.

What If Jesus Returned To Earth Just Before Election Day?

Hey, right-wing extremists—listen up and take notes.

Everyone knows that you have absolutely no use for Democrats or, worse yet, Liberals and their "radical" left-wing values. It should also be noted that, not surprisingly, you unequivocally link them to Jews (everyone knows that terms like "élitists" or "liberals" are not-so-subtle euphemisms for "Jews"). If you're correct (and when are you ever wrong?), then ponder this:

Since all Jews are either Democrats or élitist liberals, and Jesus was a Jew, were He to return to the United States on Election Day and somehow make Himself eligible to participate, how do you think He'd vote?

Chapter 7 –

When You Really Think About It...

You Shouldn't Kiss A Catholic In Winter

The deductive process of using logical reasoning to reach an indisputable conclusion does not always work. Statement "A" can be absolutely factual and true; so can statement "B". That doesn't mean that Statement "C" must be the result. To wit:

(A) Approximately one billion people worldwide get winter colds.

(B) There are approximately one billion Catholics worldwide.

(C) Therefore, every person in the world who gets a winter cold is Catholic.

You're Actually Capturing A Piece Of History

All of you are surprised by what you encounter on your latest vacation trip to the Denver area. Dozens of new developments of expensive houses, some with just a few feet of land between them, now blight the landscape. Worse yet, heading west along Route 70, the unsullied views of the Rockies you remember from just ten years ago are now interrupted by still more McMansions that dot the terrain like a bad case of measles. You're so glad you had your camera with you then, and you smile a bit ironically as you reach for your camera now.

Back from vacation, you're enjoying the wedding reception; this and funerals seem to be the only time friends and family get together. Gosh, how everyone's changed! Aunt Pearl must be in her upper nineties now, yet still fashionably dressed and able to get around on her own. You remember that black-and-white photo Uncle Max took of her in that then-stylish dress over eighty years ago. Boy, things sure change over time. Hey, there's Megan and…wait a minute. Are *both* of those kids hers? When you took that picture of Scott, he was just a few months old; now he's got a three-year-old sister. And will you look at Manny. The last time you saw him his voice was changing; now he's getting ready to begin his second year of college. You get your camera ready.

This summer of 2001 has been one of the best ever, but now you have to organize all those vacation and party photos and put them into an album. Well, not a problem; you can get to that in two weeks when the kids go back to school. Meanwhile, you have to buy more film because Labor Day weekend is coming up, and you promised to take the kids to the World Trade Center.

Just What *Is* A Retiree Or A Volunteer?

We called Bob on New Year's Day to exchange good wishes for the New Year. The unusual level of frenetic energy in his voice mandated that we inquire what was going on. Turns out he was really anticipating his next birthday, a milestone.

"Hey, guys, I'll be sixty! Just think: less than four months, and I can retire. I'm down to counting weeks—just 16 left—and when April 1st hits, I'll be counting down the last 21 days. Can you believe it? Oh, I'll probably stay on until May 1st, but then that's it—I'm free! I can do what I want with my time." He was ecstatic.

Bob's wife made him a wonderful birthday party and, true to his word, he left his job early in May. Because of schedule conflicts on both sides we didn't get together until late August, by which time we could hardly wait to find out how they were enjoying their new life and what Bob was doing with all this free time.

"Oh, I'm helping out at that big department store downtown—you know, the one that opened up in late May, in the new mall?"

We knew the behemoth to which he referred. "Hey, that's great to hear! What do you do there?"

He shrugged. "Oh, I kind of help restock and arrange goods on the racks and shelves in the men's clothing section."

"That's interesting," I said, with curiosity. "How many hours do you give them in a typical week?"

"Oh," he replied, "I'm only there three days a week—24, maybe 25 hours. And they're pretty flexible on hours."

I was confused. "Umm, I don't understand," I said, truthfully. "You're volunteering three days a week to help out at a department store? Why? What's the attraction?"

He shook his head. "Welllll, actually, I'm not volunteering; I get paid for what I do. It's part-time work, but the extra income doesn't hurt and, besides, I work enough hours to get medical benefits."

Such incidents are becoming increasingly common for reasons ranging from financial need to boredom. Fine; nothing wrong with that, except those people aren't retired; all they've done is change jobs or professions. "Retired" means no longer gainfully employed. Sure, there can be exceptions, like being summoned or subsequently selected for jury duty. One is compensated, but such activities are rare and not by choice, and the income generated probably wouldn't pay the electric bill for one month. As long as one's time is spent without receipt or expectation of remuneration that person's retired, regardless of the type of activity or degree of indulgence.

By the way, the same rule applies to volunteers who give of their time for a cause, and we know a few such good-hearted people. But there are some who help out for a couple of hours or so knowing full well that in exchange for their efforts they will be given free meals, or free tickets to an event, or discounts on merchandise and so on. Such people may be useful to these organizations, but they are not volunteers and have no right to describe themselves as such.

Why *Was* Little Black Sambo Killed?

The youngster was trapped in the woods by a group of tigers that were threatening to eat him. He tried to talk the beasts out of it and pleaded with them to free him but they were unyielding. Although terrified, the boy began to think of ways to avoid becoming their dinner and soon came up with a plan: it was a very hot day and he began running around a tree, challenging the tigers to try and catch him. They gave chase, but the shrewd lad quickly climbed the tree and sat on a branch, watching the animals racing faster and faster as they circled below, looking for him. It did not take long in that heat for the tigers to melt into butter, which the victorious lad gathered up in a pail, brought home and gave to his mother, who promptly made him delicious pancakes and served them with fresh butter.

The hero's name was Sambo, and he appeared to be only about eight or nine years old, judging by the illustrations in the book. I was awed because

I was just about the same age when I first read of his adventure in the mid-1940s and wondered whether I could have come up with such a clever life-saving solution. I so admired him.

The fact that he was a Negro meant nothing special to me; he could have been a Zuni, Eskimo, Mexican, Oriental—hell, he could have been a Martian or even a Caucasian! Growing up, my parents made certain that racial and cultural differences were understood, respected and admired, never merely tolerated and certainly never disparaged. To them, and eventually to us, the world consisted of only two kinds of people, the good and the bad. This was especially significant at a time when World War II was still raging. At that time, living in New York City, my best friend was black, and one of the girls on whom I had a crush was Chinese. I was enchanted reading *"The Arabian Nights,"* delighted seeing Walt Disney's *"Song of the South,"* warmed and amused by weekly radio shows such as *"Life with Luigi,"* The Goldbergs,*"* *"Amos 'n Andy,"* *"The Life of Riley"* and the *"Allen's Alley"* portion of *"The Fred Allen Show."* No one regarded the characters portrayed as stereotypical, offensive, ethnically negative or derisive. Hey, for how many years did Eddie Anderson fracture radio and television audiences as the butler Rochester on *"The Jack Benny Show"*? And who wasn't impressed several times a week by the intelligent, loyal and skillful Tonto, the "faithful Indian companion" of *"The Lone Ranger"*?

That's why it was both surprising and disappointing to so many of us when such amiable characters disappeared, victims of a well-intended but perhaps overly sensitive race-conscious society. In retrospect, I'm still puzzled. These beloved standards of radio and television allowed us to witness and share the day-to-day problems of ordinary people everywhere and understand the commonality of their concerns, regardless of ethnicity. They were all Americans, whether fighting for justice or struggling to raise decent kids, keep their families together and improve their lives in the face of burgeoning economic hardship and social inequity. If such qualities and values produced negative impressions of immigrants and minorities then, imagine what kind of impressions today's viewers of any television channel's "evening news" program are left with.

You Really *Are* A Role Model

Recently, a prominent musical icon got into trouble for trashing a hotel room and being involved in a brawl. Such incidents happen with almost monotonous regularity but this one got my attention. When it was pointed out that this act had disappointed his devoted fans and followers who looked up to him and held him in such awe, his response was something like "Hey, look, I'm not a role model."

Hate to tell ya, guy, but you're wrong; each of us is a role model. How you are seen by people determines what they think of you and others they associate with you, whether you're two miles or two continents away from home. Just think of your own reactions to situations or experiences. You arrived late last night, so this is your first morning in an unfamiliar city. Walking along the street, you try asking someone for directions. That person is friendly and tries his utmost to be helpful, even stopping someone else to get you that information. What's your opinion about that person? What do you think of the second person? You can virtually guarantee that this experience will create an instinctive positive gut feeling about the city and its people. If the pleasantries and niceties continue, that impression will be reinforced and probably expand to include more of that state or section of the country. In fact, were you to observe or be part of something that contradicted your perception, your first reaction would likely be to dismiss it as an uncharacteristic oddity.

And all because a stranger treated you decently. Had he or the second person you then would have been forced to ask ignored you and kept on going, or dismissed your request with a brusque "no," what do you think your response would be to people back home who asked how your trip was and what you thought about that city?

That's why how we comport ourselves matters, especially in an unfamiliar environment. It's good to hear things like, "Oh, you're from Omigosh? We've met others from there and enjoyed talking with them, too; must be a nice area." Or better yet, "You're the first person we've ever met from there who's been so pleasant." Either way you are a positive force that can initiate a reversal of negative perceptions. Just think of the times you've run into obnoxious tourists and asked someone, "Where in hell are *they* from?" and when you're told, your response is, "Yeah, that figures!"

Chapter 8 –

Something For Everyone

Two Geographic Questions For Puzzle Lovers

The mighty Mississippi River, which flows from north to south, serves as the boundary between many surrounding states. As an example, on its western side it separates Missouri and Iowa (which is above it) from Illinois, which is east of those other two states.

For your vacation this year, you have decided to follow the river's path, starting in Louisiana and driving north. Having gone through Kentucky, you have just entered southwestern Illinois. You are now on Route 3, continuing to drive north and admiring the views of the river and Missouri, both of which are to the west, on your left. You drive less than a hundred miles on Route 3 and see a sign promoting Chester, Illinois, the town where the famous comic strip and cartoon character *"Popeye"* originated. Smiling, you look once again to your left at the river to the west and the land beyond it. The river is the Mississippi, but what is the state? (Hint: it is *not* Missouri.) The answer follows the next puzzle.

It's late afternoon, and you've finished your northbound tour of the Mississippi River, which you truly enjoyed. Still having a day left before you have to head back to New York, you decide that you'd like to see more of the mid-west. So you continue driving north for about another 100 miles in Wisconsin, which is east of the Mississippi River, then cross the river into Duluth, Minnesota, where you stay the night in a motel just off Interstate 35.

The next day you get on Interstate 35 and head south through Minnesota into Iowa. You're enjoying the heartland and decide to see more of the area around Des Moines and spend the night there, since it's right near Interstate 80, which would leave you poised to begin the trip east to get home.

The next morning you get on Interstate 80, heading east. You don't have to rush home, so you decide that occasionally you'll get off I-80 and take some local highways that basically parallel I-80, see more countryside, then return to I-80. You know that to get to these local roads or back to I-80 you may have to drive a bit to the north or south before you can continue east, but you've decided that *under no circumstances* will you do any driving on a road that heads west. And you're true to your word.

You complete your eastbound drive through Iowa and enter Illinois, continuing east through Ohio, Indiana, Ohio and part of Pennsylvania before finding a motel near I-80 to spend the night. The next morning you get up and, after a light breakfast and some greatly appreciated coffee, check out and get back on I-80 heading east, arriving safely back home in New York State later that same afternoon.

It was a great vacation, but I'm curious: since you never drove on any road that headed west on your entire trip home, tell me how you managed to go through Ohio *twice*.

Let's go back to the first puzzle. (If you have an atlas or any maps handy, that will help.) As noted, the river to your left is the Mississippi, but the land beyond it is not part of the state of Missouri, so you would think that it has to be part of the state of Iowa. Surprisingly, though, it isn't; the land is actually still within the state of Illinois—Kaskaskia, Illinois, to be more precise. What happened was that some years ago, during a particularly bad flood season, the overflow of the Mississippi River actually carved out a new route just east of where it had been flowing. Rather than have to adjust or redefine the boundary between Missouri and Illinois, the decision was made to leave it as it had been—that is, continue to use the original Mississippi River boundary line that is now to the west of this newly-formed channel. And that's how you were able to look to the west across the Mississippi from Chester, Illinois into Kaskaskia, Illinois.

But what about the second puzzle? How did you manage to go through Ohio twice without ever heading west or even close to it? Well, when you entered Illinois, you continued east on I-80 for a bit; then, just past Moline, you headed northeast to local Route 92. You took it east, passing through the town of Ohio, Illinois, then continued east to local Route 89, which you took southeast back to I-80, which you rejoined and continued your trip east through the rest of Illinois, all of Indiana and Ohio and into Pennsylvania, set to continue home the next day.

Get Your "S" Out Of Bed

Some well-known names in sleeping equipment include Sealy, Serta, Simmons and Sterns & Foster; others include Select Comfort, Shandung, Sleep Number, Smithfield, South Melbourne, Spring-Aire, Stanmore, St. Mary's, Sunshine West, Surrey Hills, Sweet Dreams and Sydney. Sleepy's sells such products; even Sears used to sell them under its own name in its stores up to a few years ago.

Isn't it odd that they all begin with the letter "S"?

Location And Timing Are Everything

We were in a craft store, where my wife Barbara was looking for several "on-sale" items. Soon, apparently done, she began heading up the main aisle towards the cash registers. Suddenly, she just stopped and began looking around, with a lost expression on her face. Trying to be helpful, I inquired, "What? Anything I can do for you?" She moved closer, quickly surveyed the store once more and said, with some urgency in her voice, "I need to get felt."

Family Frivolities

Running a seasonal business was hectic enough for my father, but any economic slowdown created a whole new set of problems for him. Well-intentioned friends would assure him that "someday your ship will come in," to which my father would respond, "Yeah; and with my luck, there'll be a dock strike!"

My father had been on the telephone talking quietly and affably for a couple of minutes when suddenly, inexplicably, the volume increased and there was anger in his voice. The conversation ended abruptly, and when he joined us in the living room my mother asked what had happened. In an agitated voice Dad explained that he had given special consideration as a favor to a business associate who was now asking for more. He was silent, then just shook his head and in a somewhat exasperated voice added, "I just don't get it—you give someone a hand, and they want the whole foot!"

It was suppertime and, as always, eating was interspersed with conversation. I happened to remark that I had read a wonderful poem and liked it so much I memorized it. My father, obviously pleased, asked what the poem was. I said, *"'Abou ben Adhem,'* by Leigh Hunt."

He nodded. "Can you recite it?"

"Sure." I cleared my throat and began:

Abou ben Adhem (may his tribe increase!)
Awoke one night from a deep dream of peace
And saw, within the moonlight of his room,
Making it rich and like a lily in bloom,
An angel, writing in a book of gold…

At that point my pre-teen sister interrupted and asked, "Who's Lillian Bloom?"

Divorced from my first wife, I was in my apartment one day when my brother and his younger son, then less than ten years old, dropped in unexpectedly for a brief visit. After pleasantries were exchanged, snacks were set out and we sat around the kitchen table catching up on how things were going with our respective families, which soon turned to items of current national concern. Somehow, during the conversation, something was mentioned that elicited a comparative comment to the Norman invasion of England in 1066.

At this point my nephew, who had been listening attentively, wanted to know, "What's a Norman invasion?" My brother and I looked at each other, and when he raised his eyebrows slightly and nodded to me, I proceeded to explain.

"Well," I began, "a long time ago a group of Normans sailed on a ship from France and invaded the country of England."

"Who was the captain?" he inquired.

My brother chimed in with, "William the Conqueror."

My nephew looked puzzled. "Well, how was he able to control the ship or get anybody to do anything he asked them to do?"

I was lost. "I'm not sure I understand what you mean. Why do you think the captain would have a problem getting his men to listen to him and carry out his orders?"

My nephew perked up. "Because," he explained, "if the captain said, 'Come here, Norman, I want to talk to you,' and everyone was named Norman, how would they know which Norman the captain wanted to talk to?"

When our younger daughter was accepted for a job that required her to move to Florida, my ex-wife gave her a "going-away" party that included several local friends and neighbors. During festivities a guest and I were discussing various aspects of affirmative action, and I observed that so far it seemed to have resulted in an increase in the number of black students attending college.

My daughter happened to overhear the remark and reprovingly stated, "Dad, it's 'African-American,' not 'black'."

I turned and smiled at her, then resumed the conversation. Not too much time elapsed before I used the word "black" again.

This time the annoyance in her voice was undisguised. "Dad, I just told you, they are not called 'blacks'; the proper expression is 'African-Americans'."

I continued to look at her for a couple of seconds, then began to visually sweep the rest of the room, searching for someone specific. I finally spotted him through the doorway of an adjoining room, and called out his name. He looked around, spotted me waving at him to join us, and worked his way over through the crowd, smiling.

"Ya, good to see you, Fred," he said, that charming accent still enhancing the warmth of his voice. "What can I do for you."

"Felix," I asked, "tell me, where were you born?"

He looked surprised, but smiled and responded. "In Transvaal."

"Hmmm, Transvaal, Transvaal," I mused. "Where's that?"

His expression changed to disbelief. "Well, you know—South Africa."

I nodded and continued. "And I believe you grew up there, then came to the United States—what, some twenty years ago?"

He nodded. "Ya, that's right. Say, what's going on here?"

I persisted for one more comment. "Well, then, Felix, I guess that means you're an African-American."

He looked at me quizzically, but agreed. "Well, of course I am."

I turned my head quickly and gave my daughter a concluding "Well?" look, saying nothing. Her mouth was agape, but when she finally composed herself all that emerged was an "Oh my God" in a tone of awe that usually accompanies realization.

There was no need to remind her that Felix was white (or was he Caucasian?) or to say anything more, but I couldn't resist. "Well, so much for being politically correct."

During late May of 1995, Barbara's chorus participated in three consecutive recording sessions of Pietro Mascagni's two-act opera *"Silvano"* at SUNY Purchase in Westchester County, New York. For the first one I accompanied her and drove, since it was a 140-mile round trip from our less-than-two-year-old home and I was certain that she would rather concentrate on the music than the road.

It was late afternoon when we drove into the Performing Arts Center Theatre's huge, nearly empty parking lot and picked a space. At the same time, another car pulled into a spot just ahead of us in the next row, and we all exited our respective cars simultaneously. I knew the lady who appeared on the driver's side—like Barbara, an alto—but not the tall, rather distinguished-looking gentleman who emerged from the front passenger's side and, like the two of us, was heading towards her. When we met, greetings were exchanged and I was introduced to the man who, as it turns out, sang bass in the chorus. This was not surprising, listening to the deep, velvet timbre of his rich voice. It was a perfect accompaniment to his trim, 6-foot-plus physical appearance crowned by a meticulously groomed beard and silver hair reminiscent of Commander Whitehead, the notable spokesman for Schweppes Tonic Water commercials.

"Oh, Susan," I said, turning towards the lady, "before I forget—I haven't seen you in awhile—thank you so much for the chive plants you gave Barbara last year. She planted them and so far they're doing well. But I have to say, I thank you with mixed emotions. Because we still had a lot of outdoor work to do and our land is so rocky, I wasn't planning to start a new garden until this year. On the other hand, though, you know how much we've wanted to have a garden, so thank you for giving us the incentive to get started. It's still a relatively small area, so we decided to choose only expensive crops, so in addition to the chives last year, we planted lobsters."

Susan smiled; the gentleman fingered his beard, eyebrows raised. I looked at him and continued. "Unfortunately, none came up, so we never had any."

He studied me without smiling, as though I had just uttered the most obvious, stupid statement he'd ever heard. Then he responded thoughtfully in his most respectful, serious British manner.

"Well, of course not; lobsters are biennials!"

Since it was a second marriage for each of us, Barbara and I had a small Sunday afternoon wedding with just eight guests, followed by a reception back home. Days earlier we had ordered ample quantities and varieties of food platters, which we picked up on the morning of the wedding. Anything perishable or to be kept chilled was put in the refrigerator; other items waited patiently on the kitchen table for all of us to return about four hours later. When we did, it took just minutes to retrieve, unwrap and arrange it all on the dining room table and island counter space between the kitchen and dining room. Champagne was poured and distributed, and our best man led everyone in a toast to us with best wishes for a lifetime of love and happiness in good health. We were now ready to feast.

Well, almost ready; I still had one more thing to take care of.

One day during the prior workweek the company cafeteria had prepared a special lunch dish featuring hot chicken parts. I looked at it and an idea just hit me out of left field. I chose the dish and ate it all except one needed piece, which I wrapped in a paper napkin. To complete my plan I took a few small packets of tomato ketchup, put everything in a small paper bag and refrigerated it for the rest of the day until I was ready to head out. Once I got home (typically 20 minutes or so before Barbara) I opened the packets and squeezed all the ketchup into one very small but wide and shallow glass cup, covered the top with plastic wrap and buried it and the chicken part in the lower depths of our refrigerator. Now I was set for Sunday.

Having finished toasting and wishing us well, our guests were waiting for us to invite them to partake of food and drink, but I held up my right hand and said, "Uh, before we all start eating, there's still one more thing to be done." Everyone hesitated and looked at me; I continued. "There's an old Jewish custom that's traditionally performed during a wedding ceremony— part of our heritage—and I'd like to ask you to share this with me. It'll just take a moment."

I smiled at everyone and turned to look at Barbara, who seemed totally perplexed and unaware of what was coming next. Good! I headed towards the refrigerator, opened the door, retrieved my two treasures and unwrapped them within so nobody could see what I had. I then set the ketchup-filled cup in the palm of my left hand and picked up the chicken piece with my right hand, did an about-face and walked back to my bride. Turning to face her, I looked into her beautiful but wondering eyes, smiled and asked her to extend her right hand out towards me, palm up and open. Trusting me, she complied. I dipped the piece into the ketchup and began to smear it over her palm, repeating the procedure a few more times until it was thoroughly and deeply covered. I then raised the piece above my head for all the guests to see, looked at them seriously, and turned back to Barbara. Placing the cup on the counter space, I positioned my left hand under her covered hand and held it gently by her wrist. Gazing at her with utmost seriousness, I extended my right hand towards her as though offering her the piece of chicken and soberly declared, "WITH THIS WING, I THEE RED!"

Astonishingly, almost twenty years later, we're still married.

One Of Nature's Greatest Mysteries

It's March, so you dress sensibly for your daily walk: underwear topped by a sweatshirt, jacket, hat, gloves, scarf, warm socks, and jeans whose legs extend to barely an inch off the ground, totally obscuring a pair of new tightly-laced sneakers. You walk briskly along the side of a paved country road for awhile, then are suddenly compelled to stop because of the irritating pain centered at one point on the bottom of your foot. Cursing mildly, you stop, bend over, untie the lace of the offending sneaker and take it off, turn it upside down and shake it vigorously until a small object falls out. You see it and are almost in disbelief, especially since this has happened more than once before today; yet again, all you can think of is, *"How in hell did that pebble get into my shoe?"*

Great Expectations

We've all experienced at least one or two if not all three of the following scenarios. You're in a phone conversation, being asked, "Will you be home tomorrow?"

"Yes, I will."

1) "Oh, good; we'll send out a service technician tomorrow to check out the unit and make the necessary repairs, which should fix the problem. Let's see…yes, you're second on the list, so he should be there mid-morning, maybe early afternoon, probably sometime between 10:30 and 1:00 in the afternoon."

2) "Oh, good; we have a rush package that we were unable to deliver yesterday, but we'll be there today, sometime this morning, probably before 11:30."

3) "Oh, good; we have your new washer and dryer, and we'll be able to deliver it tomorrow. Our driver has one other stop before yours, but he should be there before noon, if that's all right."

You know the bottom line: *if* anyone even shows up that day, wanna bet it's after 4:30 P.M., perhaps as late as 6:00 P.M.?

Equal Housing Opportunities

People throughout New York State were becoming concerned in early 2007 because published statistics confirmed that an increasing number of residents were moving to other states that had lower taxes. Officials were concerned about the economic implications, particularly in such areas as lost incomes and tax revenues.

I looked into this, and to the best of my knowledge none of these state-switchers had abandoned their residences. Those who owned homes, condos or co-ops sold their places to new occupants; those in rented dwellings left when their leases expired and were replaced by new tenants. It's likely that if all these newcomers could afford their new quarters, they were also financially able to maintain them by such means as gainful employment or comfortable retirement.

So what fiscal consequences were State officials worried about?

A Real Hose Job: The Watered-Down Version

I had finished grocery shopping except for three items from the fresh produce area. Getting there, I selected a few nice vine-ripened tomatoes, a large Romaine lettuce, and was heading for the last item on my list when I spotted a lady already there, patiently waiting and watching an employee spraying a fine watery mist over the contents of the display shelf. After what seemed like a minute, he stopped. The woman then reached forward, at which point he turned to her abruptly and asked, "Can I help you?"

Caught off guard, the woman smiled nervously and responded, "Oh, I was just trying to take a leek."

The Best Legal Advice One Can Get

Part of my undergraduate business management studies included an introductory-type basic law course. The instructor (whose name, I believe, was Bartel) presented a variety of situations in a highly effective manner, achieving excellent interactive participation and, for most of us, expanded cognitive skills. Perhaps most memorable, though, was the advice he gave us within the first few minutes of the opening session, after welcoming us and introducing himself:

1) If you ever need a lawyer, go to one and explain everything simply and

honestly. If he then tells you not to worry because it's a sure winner or we can't lose, find another lawyer.

2) Anytime you make a deal, arrangement or contract, get it in writing. Forget verbal agreements, understandings or handshakes, especially when it comes to family—yes, even parents. That may sound outrageous and seem ridiculous, but some of the most angry, bitter court cases have involved such situations. Get it in writing!

What's Your Initial Reaction?

Some colleges or universities are known by a name, such as Yale or Harvard; others are known by initials, such as MIT or UCLA. Either way, though, when a new institution is being founded, one must anticipate the possible adaptation of a selected name to initials and examine the results. Many years ago, for instance, I received a Masters Degree from City College of New York, referred to as CCNY. Concurrently, a fellow worker received his Masters Degree from Stevens-Hoboken Institute of Technology.

A Flash Of Off-Color Brilliance

Eddie was an affable, soft-spoken man, smart and quick-witted. He and I were part of an eight-person van pool that picked us up at a designated location near our homes each morning and drove us some 25 miles to one of the company's two work facilities. Our driver would let three people out at the first building, then proceed to the second one, drop off the four of us, park the van and join us. At day's end, with rare exception, all four of us would be waiting by the front door, where he would pick us up and proceed to get the remaining three at the other building for the trip home. Sounds simple enough, except for one constant complication: *never* were all three first-building passengers present when the van pulled up; we always had to wait for one and usually two of them.

This was aggravating, but there really wasn't much that could be done. One of them, John, was a very dedicated worker who often had to be reminded by his fellow workers that it was time for him to catch his van ride. The second, an attractive young lady with a great figure, worked all the way in the back part of the building and was more of a meanderer than a walker. The last of the tardy trio was an unusually short fellow who was the most likely of the three to be out there on time.

One afternoon, after the four of us had been picked up, we approached the first building and were stunned at what we saw: incredibly, all three of them were there, ready and waiting. We were all speechless except for Eddie, who smiled and observed, "Well, there they are—the grunt, the cunt and the runt!"

Chapter 9 –

More Homespun Insight, Advice, Oddities, Wit And Sarcasms

1) Many people are struck by a sobering thought on June 21st. Although usually the longest day of the year, they realize that the days will be getting shorter and before they know it, winter will have arrived. However, such people are gladdened on December 21st because now the days will gradually lengthen. Can spring be far behind?

2) The ugliest car you'll see while driving is the one sitting on the soft shoulder with either its hood or trunk open.

3) These days, we live in a binary world; everything is either 0 or 1, on or off, yes or no, black or white. If you don't love something, you must hate it. There's no in-between —even gray areas have vanished. (from about 1972)

4) Autumn needs two blustery periods: one to help the trees shed their leaves and the other to blow them onto your neighbor's lawn.

5) Compared to the United Nations, FEMA (The Federal Emergency Management Association) is the most useful, effective, productive and beneficial organization ever.

6) "Hands-On Experience" was a documentary about a man whose insatiable passion was groping females of every age, but it never made it to the theaters because critics deemed it to be too blasé. But

when I had a chance to view it I thought it had lots of feeling; the male star's performance in particular was very touching.

7) When cooking, always read through an entire recipe first; it can save you time and help bypass stupidity. To give a fairly common example: why bother to "finely mince 4 large garlic cloves" rather than just chop them if they're going to be sautéed and then puréed in a blender?

8) It is better to know a little about a lot of things than to be an expert in just one area.

9) Anyone can be upset with some aspect of what's going on in government at any level and even be quite outspoken about that issue. But if someone gripes to you, just ask one question: "Did you vote in the last election?" If the answer is "no," tell that person in a nice way to piss off.

10) Never mistake the legal system for the justice system.

11) A popular radio ad begins: "Hi! This is Pat Summerall. For years I've been telling you about my Dux bed." I chime in with: "Now I'd like to tell you about my cat's litter box."

12) Never serve drinks in colored glasses, especially wines and liqueurs. Nobody wants to be handed an intensely deep ruby-red Merlot, an excitingly sparkling gin and tonic or a Scotch on the rocks in a green or blue goblet.

13) One should respect the office of President of the United States, but that doesn't necessarily include its occupant.

14) *A day without coffee is like a day without coffee.*
   —Testicles (387-314 B.C.E.)

15) Speaking of coffee, the world's best coffee is mountain-grown. So is the world's worst. It's *all* mountain-grown.

16) Many blacks frequently speak out against what they perceive as discrimination in the arts because they are not asked to portray characters traditionally considered to be white, ranging from Julius Caesar to Santa Claus. Well, I have to wonder how equality-minded these protesters would be if a film biography of Dr. Martin Luther King, Jr. were made starring Clint Eastwood or Jackie Chan.

17) What a waste! So many New York State drivers forced to spend extra money on automobile accessories that they never even use. Like directional signals.

18) I am more certain of the existence of God than I am of the apparently obvious fact that you are now reading this.

19) I just created an original car bumper sticker, but nobody seems

interested in using it. It reads, "Proud Parent of a Model Prisoner at a Minimum Security Facility."

20) Depending on whether someone views a glass with liquid in it as being half-full or half-empty supposedly classifies that person as an optimist or a pessimist. Can the same be done with a person who says that he has one leg longer than the other rather than shorter?

21) There are men who are somewhat awkward or clumsy, but I remember one poor guy who was so inept that the first time he tried to swallow Viagra it got stuck in his throat. All he got was a stiff neck.

22) We send out dozens of holiday greeting cards in December; why does it seem that the first one we receive is usually from someone not on our mailing list?

23) If the financially troubled General Motors spent just half of its advertising budget to actually improve product quality, how many more vehicles do you think they'd sell?

24) Eat raw chicken and you risk getting salmonella. What do you risk getting if you eat raw salmon?

25) Why is just any one typical Hallmark greeting card more expensive to purchase than an entire Sunday newspaper?

26) By the way, Hallmark is not alone: Ambassador recently ran ads promising that if you bought just ten of their greeting cards you would get a free Mustang convertible.

27) It's not that I'm gaining weight; I'm just simply becoming more anorexically challenged.

28) George W. Bush was our President for two terms, starting in 2000. By 2006 many were describing him as the worst President of the century, while others considered him the best. At the time, both views were accurate and correct.

29) If you want to rip someone off, don't try selling that person the Brooklyn Bridge; instead, sell him shares of stock in a French company that produces deodorants.

30) A Republican is a Democrat whose family reached middle- or upper-class status under Democratic leadership and is now rich enough to be a Republican.

31) Christians spending money carefully or wisely are admired for being thrifty, frugal, prudent, economical or, at worst, parsimonious. So why is it that Jews who practice the same financial restraint are viewed as being tight-fisted, miserly, niggardly, skinflints or, at best, cheapskates?

32) The number of citizens in our nation who are economically

challenged is increasing rapidly, but what can they do? Simple; they can just pack up and move to some third-world country, give up their citizenship and apply to the U.S. for foreign aid.

33) These days it's almost impossible to see an infant up to two years old without a pacifier in its mouth. Do you wonder why so many of them begin to indulge in oral sex in their early teens?

34) So you want to be rich and famous? That's easy; just do something highly unethical, immoral, salacious, criminal or merely reprehensible on a level that gains national attention. Be assured, in no time at all you will be offered your choice of the most lucrative book and movie deals.

35) Many celebrities earn tens of millions of dollars each year. So why do so many mature ones wear dentures that either produce sibilant speech sounds or are so visually obvious that one can't help but wonder if they bought them on sale at Wal-Mart?

36) It's not that some priests abuse altar boys, they just use them for religious purposes—that is, they pray on them. I guess that's what makes them lay priests.

37) Be it ever so humble, there's no place like a chateau on the French Riviera.

38) In the mid-1930s the U.S. government came up with a simple nine-digit hyphenated numerical system to identify each and every one of the hundred-plus-million persons in the country (it was called "Social Security Number"). So why do today's financial, credit card or other presumably efficient computer-based organizations need over a dozen numbers and/or characters to achieve the same results?

39) There's a huge difference between a "Woman," with a capital "W," and a "woman," who is nothing more than an adult female member of her species—like a tarantula.

40) Nobody's perfect—hell, even I have to wear glasses.

41) Sometimes a person needs a new vehicle but can't afford one. If he's looking for a good, solid, reliable means of transportation he should buy a certified "used car" from a reputable Japanese car dealer; otherwise, let him purchase a prestigious "previously-owned automobile" elsewhere and settle for hoping to impress his friends.

42) Lots of people have stated openly that George W. Bush is arguably the nation's worst President ever, but many others have objected strongly to that statement, and I must agree with them. In this case, the word "arguably" should never be used.

43) Do any couples ever produce babies that are anything but cute, lovely, adorable or beautiful?

44) We've all seen television ads for a product that typically is not available in stores, with an announcer enthusiastically describing its features, but be careful: if he then says anything like "And the price? Far less than you might expect to pay for...", forget it; be assured that it will cost more than you could ever imagine in your wildest dreams.

45) We've also seen "personal" newspaper ads—you know, for "Men Seeking Women" or "Women Seeking Men," "Men Seeking Men," "Women Seeking Women." Well, I tried putting an ad in our local paper for "Men Seeking Sheep" but they thought that was weird, until I convinced them that of course I was only interested in female sheep.

46) Millions of people like the idea of an SUV but find it too damned big; it's like driving a truck. Oooh, auto makers: wait—I just had an idea. What if you built a smaller, more stylish, fuel-efficient version that anybody—maybe even families—would really go for? I can even think of a good name for it. You could call it "a station wagon."

47) To ask a Jew on Yom Kippur day, "What are you having for lunch?" is like that same Jew asking God to "Give us this day our daily bread" during Passover.

48) The government assumes that, because of fewer benefits claims, "unemployment declined last month," implying an improving economy with more new jobs. But what if the fewer claims were because, for some, the time to continue collecting unemployment benefits simply ran out?

49) I don't know of anyone who's afraid to be caught alone at night on a dimly lit street in a bad part of the city because he might be mugged or shot at by a gang of gays.

50) The phone rings. You answer it and are surprised to hear the voice of someone you haven't heard from for awhile. Turns out everything's OK, but you're curious: why call now, after such a long time? It doesn't take long to find out. When the caller says something like, "Oh, by the way, while I have you on the phone...," it's obvious: they need something you have or can do for them.

51) I so admire anyone who can set aside grief or pain for loss suffered just hours ago in a mishap to find the strength to initiate a multi-million-dollar lawsuit against the cause.

Chapter 10 -

No, I'm Not Running Out Of Breadth

Irony, Fate, Destiny—What Does That Mean?

We've stopped along Route 28, probably the most scenic of the very few roads that traverse New York State's beautiful Adirondack Mountains. In nearly three hours of cruising we've only seen two cars, both going in the opposite direction. This is a lovely, lonely two-lane ribbon of gently curving concrete offering a series of gradual descents into river-lined woods and farmlands, matched by corresponding rises to isolated heights of rocks and trees. It's a perfect summer day, a "photographer's day," with the deep blue sky punctuated by several large three-dimensional puffy white clouds, beneath which lie the waves of smooth-topped mountains protecting their snug, secure valleys of variegated trees and crops. Standing at the edge of the road in a warm breeze we scan the horizon, miles away, and absorb the vista before us: a tapestry of virtually limitless land, with just one insignificant and undisciplined thread running through it. I get ready to use my camera, but I know that my attempt to interpret such a creation on film will be like Arachne expecting her weaving efforts to compete with the work of the goddess Aurora.

Awed, we get back into the car and continue. The road ahead is visible for about a quarter of a mile but then seems to vanish—a subtle way of announcing another descent into the next series of valleys. But there's also something ahead in the road which, as we approach it, becomes more recognizable. It's a groundhog that's been run over.

Four years later, in July of 1969, man lands on the moon for the first time ever. It's an incredible event. Statisticians calculate that the chances of success for such an unlikely occurrence are comparable to the probability of a marksman aiming a .22-calibre rifle at a target and hitting the exact center of the bull's-eye in one shot from thirteen miles away. One can only imagine what the odds would be that a small animal trying to cross an infrequently-traveled road that's less than forty feet wide and surrounded by tens of thousands of acres would be killed in the attempt.

Zubin Mehta Enjoys A Concert

The lobby of Lincoln Center's Avery Fisher Hall was filled that evening with well-dressed patrons whose conversations created a collective atmosphere of excited anticipation. "Oh, I just *love* the Ninth Symphony! With the singing, it just *has* to be Beethoven's best." "…being done by the Philharmonic with Mehta conducting? I wouldn't have missed this for anything." "I know; we were lucky to have a subscription. I'll tell you, this concert sold out so quickly that…" "Well, maybe, but since Toscanini, who else can do the Beethoven Ninth with more drive or…" "Believe it or not, I actually heard this chorus that's doing the 'Ode to Joy' tonight sing once before. They sang—I think it was a Bach Double Chorus, I'm not sure—they sang here a few years ago, and they were really good. In fact Gretchen even said that she had never heard…"

My heart swelled with pride at that last statement, because the gentleman who made it was absolutely correct. However, only I knew that my Barbara was an alto with this chorale that had been chosen again to perform in New York City's famed cultural center. Weaving my way through the ticket-holders, I couldn't wait for the concert to begin. Happily, it wasn't that long before the lights began flickering rhythmically, silently beckoning the "lobbyists" to enter the concert hall, be given their programs and find their seats. Sitting approximately in the middle of the orchestra section, just right of center, I scanned the stage area, trying to find my baby, based on where she said she would be. Ah, there she was, looking so lovely and, in turn, inconspicuously trying to spot my location. Sticking to my customary tradition in these circumstances I stood up slowly, stretched and waved slightly. When she nodded her head in recognition and smiled at me, I gave her a grinning "thumbs-up" in return and sat down. We were now ready for the concert to begin, and when the maestro emerged and headed for the podium to lively applause we figured he was, too.

The first three movements, not surprisingly, were energetic, well paced, and played with the usual ensemble-like precision that New Yorkers take for granted but few orchestras worldwide can match. The audience was enjoying the concert but, as always, awaited its favorite part—the last movement, which, with a brief frenetic flurry of musical activity announcing its beginning, was now under way.

It didn't take long for the familiar "Ode to Joy" theme to emerge and strengthen with repetition, leading to the vocal entries of the bass soloist, chorus and remaining vocalists. The piece was flowing well and had reached the point about halfway through where the musical intensity eases and hesitates momentarily, as if Beethoven was trying to find an even more effective way to make his point. He succeeded, using the orchestra to accent the fervor and passion of the chorus as it began the high point of the movement:

Freude, schöner Götterfunken   (Joy, thou source of light immortal,
Tochter aus Elysium...   Daughter of Elysium...

And then it happened: Zubin Mehta stepped back, leaned against the podium's protective rail, crossed his legs while casually folding his arms across his chest, relaxed and became a very pleased observer. With no diminution of excellence, the performance continued without his participation until the verse concluded over half a minute later, at which point he took over and directed the remainder of the work.

At the end, the audience began to applaud modestly, which Mehta and the four soloists acknowledged with polite bows before exiting the stage. The applause then lessened somewhat and did not increase noticeably even as the conductor returned, followed by the soloists, and headed alone to the podium.

Turning to the crowd, Mehta again bowed; the applause level increased appreciably. He continued to bow, then extended his right arm towards the soloists clustered a few feet from him. They bowed and, curiously, the rate of applause slowed and the level dropped significantly. This continued until they stopped bowing and looked towards Mehta, who once again bowed to increasing applause. He then turned and directed the orchestra to stand; the applause became even more enthusiastic. He waited, letting the orchestra enjoy the audience's sincere tribute. As they sat down, Mehta pointed to the chorale seated behind them and motioned for them to stand up, at which point the audience went wild. The clapping intensity and volume increased instantly to maximum decibel level, yet was actually overpowered by the shouts, cheers, bravos and whistles of a crowd that had risen as one to its feet and was unrelenting in its praise for almost a full minute. They were joined by many of the Philharmonic's musicians in the string sections, tapping their bows on their instruments or music stands and their feet on the stage floor. The maestro himself was applauding, smiling and nodding his head. The chorale was still on its feet, blushing collectively and clearly overcome. Smiling shyly, some glanced down or at each other, but soon all were acknowledging the orchestra and the audience.

Back in the lobby, the audience still bubbled with excitement and enthusiasm as it headed for the exits. "Omigod, when they began singing that part,…" "…but that chorus! I'm telling you, I got goose-bumps when they began the…" "I hate to have to tell them what a concert they missed; maybe it was recorded…" "…yeah, the soloists were mediocre, but *that choir*—I mean, talk about fabulous singing…" Soon, over half the crowd had left, making it easy to spot my love when she entered, radiant and still in formal attire. Reaching her, I just embraced her. "Wow! What a night! You guys were so great! What a night! Wow!" It was all I could say, but she understood; both of us were still awed by this evening. What a night! What a perceptive audience!

Mozart Simply Couldn't Handel It

Noted conductor Gerard Schwarz initiated the "Mostly Mozart Festival" in New York City some years ago, which went on to enjoy great success. One of these concerts included Mozart's "Messiah," a strange piece that seemed to be little more than a translation into German of Händel's immortal masterpiece. But for a few scattered personal touches, the music and style were unmistakably Händel's.

Barbara's chorale had been selected to perform this work at that concert in Lincoln Center's Avery Fisher Hall, with the maestro himself conducting. Sitting in the fourth row of the balcony, it was gratifying to see that virtually every seat in the house was occupied. Searching the stage area I found my sweetie and, as always, stood up so she would know where I was. Soon the lights dimmed, the maestro appeared to enthusiastic applause, and the concert began.

The music filled the hall, enjoyed by an audience that was both knowledgeable and appreciative. The sections flowed well, and it wasn't long before more than half of the oratorio had been sung. It was time for the beloved "Hallelujah" chorus.

The orchestra began with the familiar first few introductory bars in a perky, lively tempo, alerting the concert-goers. Then the chorus joined them with an exuberant, robust "Haaaa leh loo ya," during which a few devoted traditionalists in the balcony rose to their feet and stood tall and erect, arms extended downward so that the hands met and crossed, covering the groin area. At this point, a few urgent whispers could be heard throughout the balcony, asynchronously articulating the same command: "Sit down, sit down!" Bewildered, all the standees sat down over the next few seconds—all, that is, but one very proper-looking gentleman, probably in his sixties. He continued to stand unmoved, head slightly raised, eyes unblinking, presenting a most noble image. Further whisperings were proving to be ineffective. Suddenly, a low but authoritative voice spoke up:

"Siddown, stupid! It's Mozart, not Händel; it's in German!"

Slowly, his dignity slightly shaken by the words and the muffled giggles of the audience, the gentleman complied.

The Wrong Time To Be Bad In Math

First National City Bank (now Citibank) on 53rd Street and Park Avenue in New York City was a nice place to work in the early days of computers. As a systems analyst, challenging projects were always waiting for our group.

One involved computerizing of various interest calculations as part of a larger financial streamlining effort. To emphasize the significance of this effort, the project team was assembled in our conference room for a brief lecture, which included the importance of accurate timely computations. The genial speaker announced that he had a question for us, and proceeded.

"Say you deposited one dollar in a savings account back in 1664, and it earned five per cent interest, compounded daily. Now it's 1964, 300 years later. How much money do you think would be in that bank account today?"

Most of our group members picked up pencils and began setting down a series of calculations on paper. Not being a math wizard, I sat there trying to figure out how to attack this problem when the answer suddenly hit me. I raised my hand; the speaker noticed.

"Yes," he said, smiling and pointing at me. "How much money would you have?"

"Nothing," I answered, confidently. "Everything would have probably been lost in 1933, when so many banks failed and the rest closed because of the Great Depression."

Turns out that was not exactly the answer he was looking for.

Why Do Sports Still Continue To Compare Apples To Oranges?

Competitive activities can be a wonderful thing for everyone: the participants, the loyal fans or spectators and the very activity itself. The pursuit of the impossible—perfection—often results in the achievement of excellence. Yes, there are downsides, ranging from an inability to perform well that day to failure to even "make the grade." However, such results still should be appreciated because it does take a high level of self-esteem, courage or even misguided arrogance to have tried in the first place, especially in sports, where a performance is sometimes measured over an entire season.

Throughout the ages, sports have been created with parameters and rules, acknowledging and rewarding those participants whose outstanding performances have exceeded existing standards. This in turn has motivated and even compelled future competitors to strive to exceed these newest accomplishments, thus constantly "raising the bar." This is at it should be. As more competitions become global, there is a greater need for athletes to train more creatively or develop more effective performance techniques. Two examples of this come to mind:

In the 1930s and '40s, Johnny Weissmuller was perhaps the most famous "Tarzan" of all the actors who portrayed the famous Edgar Rice Burroughs hero in movies. He was also an Olympic athlete, a beautiful swimmer. Watching his steady, unwavering streamlined strokes as he raced through waters at incredible speed was almost unbelievable. Weissmuller's technique was standard for that time: when he extended his left arm his head turned to the right, emerged from the water and maybe took in or exhaled air. Then, as his left arm retreated, it was his right arm that lunged forward as his head swung synchronously leftward, face momentarily submerged, then reappeared. This "head-left, head-right; head-left, head-right" procedure was standard in those days; he was fluidity personified.

Today, swimmers keep their heads face down in the water for long periods, churning ahead with many "left-arm, right-arm; left-arm, right-arm" cycles before picking up their heads to expel stale air and inhale deeply to repeat the process with heads submerged. It is, apparently, a good technique that produces even greater speed.

A second example involves baseball or softball. Until Astroturf was born, being a shortstop or third baseman meant that when a ground ball was hit your way you charged forward and went after it, crouching low and turned slightly sideways. Scooping up the ball with your gloved hand you removed it with your other hand while still in motion and threw the ball sideways or overhand to first base to get the batter out. Now those infielders wait for the ball to come to them before scooping it up and firing to first base, remaining set in place. This makes the throw more forceful, which may be needed because it's also longer in distance; however, since even youngsters playing sandlot ball today seem to prefer the latter method, perhaps it is a better or more accurate way to handle an infield grounder.

Achieving better results through creative adaptation of standard performance practices is not only acceptable, it is laudable. The same is true of racers and marathon runners who seek to improve their endurance by training at high altitudes in the mountains where the air is thinner, making ground-level performance relatively easy. Such new approaches are the result of the ability to review prior performances and see ways to do better, given the same judging parameters. What is totally deplorable, though, is the continued use of the same evaluation process for a sport in which established guidelines, rules and procedures have changed, thus unfairly setting new standards while, worse yet, relegating past champions to undeserved obscurity. Again, here are two cases in point:

In the 1963 NFL season, Jim Brown of the Cleveland Browns set a rushing record of 1,863 yards, which lasted until O. J. Simpson of the Buffalo Bills broke it in 1974, rushing for 2,003 yards. It was quite an accomplishment; however, Brown's record might still be standing if pro football hadn't increased the total number of games played in a season from 12 to 16 within those eleven years.

A similar event happened in major league baseball. In the 1927 season, "Babe" Ruth of the Yankees hit an unimagined 60 home runs, a record that held up until 1961 when Roger Maris, another Yankee, broke it by slamming 61. This triggered a furor and caused him much emotional pain from many baseball fans who saw him as the villain who toppled the heroic Bambino. Yet the new record was established, in spite of the fact that the number of games played in a season had only recently been increased from 154 to 162, and Maris had struck the 60th and 61st blows within those last newly-added eight games. Worse yet, let's not forget that the 1927 record was set in the new Yankee Stadium, "The House that Ruth Built," with its right-field stands much closer to home plate than the left-field seats. This was done deliberately to favor the left-handed slugger who, as a Yankee, played half the season there, giving him, shall we say, the "home-field advantage." As a Yankee, Maris not only benefited also from this break, along with the extra eight games, but also had the advantage of his era's "livelier" baseball.

While changes in other sports may not be as extreme, they're constant. For instance, how many golfers make longer drives or more accurate subsequent shots these days because of new clubs made of materials and technology that never existed half a century ago? And how about pole vaulters? How can a record set years ago by a champion using a simple wooden pole be challenged now by someone using a fiberglass-type pole that's so flexible it virtually propels him over the bar? With such a pole, of course the bar can be set much higher, leading to more new records, but where does it end? Years from now, what if a young vaulter runs towards the bar, and as his speed reaches seven miles an hour a small rocket that he has strapped around each ankle becomes active and launches him an unprecedented 207 feet into the air, just clearing the bar? If no one has ever even approached such a tremendous performance, does this set the new standard?

Sometimes We All Jump To Conclusions

You're blindfolded and standing among a group of pleasantly chatting people. You have no idea where you are or what's going on, but it soon becomes obvious that you're outdoors at some kind of social gathering. You'd like to find out more but, being unable to see, all you can do is use your other senses to help. Whatever is going on, it doesn't take long to pick up the unmistakable aromas of several delicious foods being prepared and the tinkling of glassware and china. A wedding reception? Maybe it's a graduation party, or a July Fourth celebration or neighborhood get-together.

Suddenly, a nearby voice to your right calls out, "Hey, Phil, can we go look at that car tomorrow?"

The surprised response comes from your left. "Charlie, aren't we going golfing with the guys tomorrow?"

Okay, I know what this is going to sound like but let's be honest: what kind of images comes to mind? It's easy to imagine a well-dressed crowd of people surrounding you, probably middle or upper class. Perhaps you were transported to a country club or a golf club.

Now let's change the response by just one word: "Charlie, aren't we going bowling with the guys tomorrow?"

What kind of images spring to mind now?

Extremists And Terrorist Bombers

It seems that every day in the news the conflict in Iraq has some variation of the same horrible tragedy: a car bomber drives into a crowd of people and detonates the explosives, killing anywhere from fewer than 10 people to well over 120. At this rate, one has to wonder whether Iraq will run out of cars first or people.

Letters Written By Civil War Soldiers

History has preserved thousands of examples from the Civil War of correspondence between lonely, anxious soldiers at war and their concerned families back home. I'm pretty sure that we've all seen or heard wonderful examples of these treasures, whether in subject-specific books, museum collections, readings or television specials. Most possess a beautiful flowing style of expressive eloquence that can easily transport one back in time to the writer's world, revealed perhaps with understated emotion but undisguised and unabashed simplicity. And it's all there for us to absorb, to feel, to remember.

How did they do it? Aside from military commanders, the vast majority of troops on both sides were just ordinary men—farmers, blacksmiths, carpenters, peddlers, shop workers, youngsters—who, in addition to their work, had to maintain their land, its buildings, animals and equipment, as well as protect, provide for and help raise families. Many from remote areas had never attended school or, if they had, left after seventh or eighth grade to work and help keep the family going. Some that had gone probably were lucky enough to complete the equivalent of high school. But in all cases, these were just everyday, relatively young men; how were they able to develop and master such impressive writing skills that usually come with further education, advancing years or natural ability? How did they do it?

One Aspect Of Reckless Driving Clarified

Arriving at work today, Steve greeted me with the usual "Hey, how's it going?", to which I replied, "Pretty good, except for the idiot who pulled out of his driveway onto Forest Avenue right in front of me on my way to work this morning. Pretty reckless."

He looked at me for a couple of seconds, then asked, "Did you have to hit the brakes?" I responded "No."

He smiled. "Then it wasn't reckless. A friend of mine's a cop, and I once told him about a similar situation that happened to me and he explained the difference. He said that if you have to take your foot off the gas pedal and apply the brakes, then what the guy in front of you did was reckless. But if all you had to do was take your foot off the gas pedal to stop accelerating, then the guy had left enough distance between you so that what he did wasn't reckless."

I thought about it and nodded in agreement. I think the officer had made a valid and very good distinction.

The Hardest Job In The World

If a woman chooses to enter the professional or business world and strive for a successful career, that's great, and she should never be discouraged or discriminated against (or favored) because of her gender. The same is true for those who have no choice and have to work because of unexpected economic or family troubles. Either way, these are women doing what they want to do or have to do, and I certainly admire and support their efforts. My problem is with the large number of women who plunged into the Women's Lib movement of the 1960s and immediately swam to the point of its extremes. They felt they needed a more meaningful self-controlled life, to get out into the world and taste the joy of divorce-induced freedom and know the excitement of being part of the workforce and being challenged by job demands. They simply had to be more than mere stay-at-home soccer moms or housewives.

Are they kidding? There isn't a more challenging, crucial job in the world, and any man who refuses to admit that or, worse yet, belittles it ought to be shot. How many skills does a woman have to employ every day just to be a good parent, never mind being a wife, lover, friend, supporter, psychologist and partner to her husband? Can any executive create and operate a successful home without being a planner, organizer, financial wizard, shopper, creative chef, maid, servant, cleanup crew, chauffeur, social secretary, telephone service, nurse, teacher, disciplinarian and more? And then there's participation in community, family, social and religious activities (forget personal indulgences such as crafts or hobbies, time permitting). If paid, this lady would be worth $250,000 a year.

Yes, there are women who can manage work and parenting, but these are atypical and usually involve compromises. Dropping kids off at a $1,500-a-month day care center, for example, may provide watchful care, but what have they lost? Perhaps the chance to grow up in a loving *home* environment—like these working moms themselves did. Being a successful parent also extends beyond the home. After all, if well-raised, educated and cared-for kids aren't our nation's hope and future, what is?

Being a good mom has to be more gratifying than working for some dork or killing herself to keep up with the Joneses.

Of Course There Are Miracles

Possessing the most powerful and best military forces on earth, the greatest nation in the world was defied, challenged and fought against by a weak fledgling upstart group of connected colonies consisting primarily of farmers, slaves and a few aristocrats. Incredibly, they triumphed.

Now these former colonies had to transform themselves into one united nation, based on the principle of religious freedom without government intervention and dedicated to the proposition that all men are created equal and endowed by their Creator with certain unalienable rights such as life, liberty and the pursuit of happiness. All of these unprecedented and possibly unrealistic objectives had to be defined, detailed, discussed, debated and written, reviewed, revised, resubmitted, revamped, rewritten and made acceptable for all to admire, accept, approve, authorize, autograph and activate. As if this wasn't enough, the new country also faced urgent matters it had to address quickly and resolve correctly if it was to survive and flourish. Needs ranged from establishing military forces to banking and justice systems to international trade and diplomacy agreements and literally dozens of others. It was overwhelming. That's when George Washington, Thomas Jefferson, James Madison, John and Samuel Adams, Benjamin Franklin, Alexander Hamilton, James Madison, Patrick Henry and many others emerged, *all at the same time,* and pulled it off. We were on our way to becoming the greatest nation in the world.

Just a series of lucky coincidences? I don't think so.

For Insurance Purposes

Many museums (musea?) do not allow any indoor photography. Whenever I'd ask a docent or guard why, the response invariably would be, "Well, for insurance purposes." When I said that I didn't understand and asked them to explain I would be told that pictures could be used to study objects and produce copies or duplicates.

If that's true and it's such a threat, then why am I able to visit the museum's gift shop and purchase an incredibly detailed miniature replica or picture postcard of the item I wanted to photograph?

Why Does A Squirrel Cross The Road?

You're driving along a road; it could be in the suburbs or the country. There's nobody in back of you, in front of you, or coming from the opposite direction. Yours is the only car visible, and it's been that way for a minute or so. Suddenly, just ahead, out of nowhere, a squirrel dashes out from the right side directly across the path of your oncoming car. As your foot instinctively goes for the brake the critter's speed increases as it continues its life-threatening race to the other side. Fortunately, this time, the squirrel makes it.

I'd seen this happen more than once, but could never figure out why they would do something so risky. Were they being distracted, inattentive, careless or just plain stupid? Then, one day, while out on a walk, I saw it happen again, and the answer came to me: I now knew why squirrels cross the road. It was a rite of passage.

As with all species, they too must pass a test to prove they can handle the responsibilities and challenges of mature squirrelhood, and this is that test. If one is struck while running, or starts and then simply freezes for a second, spins around and retreats, he fails the test. If another pauses, glances around uncertainly for an instant but then bolts ahead and reaches the other side he passes, albeit not very convincingly. But the one that unhesitatingly runs the course with determination, strength and commitment, finishing with no letup in speed—well, to paraphrase Kipling, "Then yours is the earth, and the fullness thereof; and what is more, you'll be a squirrel, my son."

An Appreciation Of Inanimate Animate Objects

Never trivialize good animated art. In most cases real talent is needed to produce a meaningful drawing, regardless of who created it or why. Didn't we all grow up with superheroes and villains and Mickey Mouse and Bugs Bunny? How many political cartoons have we glanced at and known who was being satirized even before reading their text because we could recognize the main subject? How many suspects have been apprehended because a "police sketch artist" was somehow able to create a reasonably accurate representation based solely on a series of hazy descriptions and conflicting recollections given by dazed witnesses or upset victims? Have you ever been reading a "Classics Illustrated" comic book or a "Prince Valiant" comic strip and paused just to take in the beauty and detail of the people and background of one outstandingly presented panel? Such creations, to me, are far more representative of true art than paintings of soup cans or those so-called masterpieces consisting of squiggly lines made by paint-drenched worms crawling across a blank canvas.

Which Came First, The Chicken Or The Egg?

It's a silly question that's often used as an example of a situation involving choices, none of which can be selected decisively as the correct one. Ridiculous! If common sense can't supply the answer, or for those who truly don't know or simply can't figure it out, I suggest checking the Bible, Volume I (a.k.a. The Old Testament), Page 1 (probably), Chapter I ("Genesis"), Verses 20 through 23, from which excerpts are presented here (as published in Boston by B. B. Mussey in 1845):

"And God said, Let the waters bring forth abundantly the moving creature that hath life, and fowl that may fly above the earth in the open firmament of heaven. And God created...every winged fowl after his kind:...And God blessed them, saying, Be fruitful, and multiply,...and let fowl multiply in the earth. And the evening and the morning were the fifth day."

Whatever Happened To Good Ol' Molestation?

There was a time when a person making unwanted or annoying sexual advances towards someone (adult or child) was said to be molesting that person; stronger terms were reserved for describing attempted or successful assaults. These days, a guy can be accused of anything from harassment to sexual abuse and made to take sensitivity training courses just for telling a co-worker he's known for years that she really looks good in the outfit she's wearing today. The term "molesting" seems to have vanished, which is truly unfortunate because it was both accurate and appropriate.

But then again, it's not the only gem lost to the language. Does anyone remember the inimitably descriptive word "bodacious"?

Two Things Hollywood Has Failed To Do Right

Tens of thousands of movies have been made over the past 115-or-so years. Many contain spectacular, incredible special effects, most of which were painstakingly created without the use of digital technology or recent high-tech innovative devices. Yet somehow, astonishingly, two scenarios seem beyond the ability of filmmakers to simulate accurately: violinists and binocular views.

1) It's a romantic scene in which two lovers are in a Gypsy restaurant. Not unexpectedly, a violinist suddenly appears at their table and begins to serenade them. Or maybe it's a musical such as "Fiddler on the Roof," in which a violinist sits on top of a house playing the plaintive, haunting melodic theme of the story. Then again it might be a drama such as "Rhapsody," in which Elizabeth Taylor is smitten with a classical violinist, who performs frequently throughout the film. Whatever the story line or situation, it doesn't matter—regardless of how skilled or deft the actor is, *not one* has ever been able to even approximate playing a violin convincingly, especially if you watch the actor's

pathetic use of the bow. Pianists, other musicians, fine; but the portrayal of a credible fiddler seems impossible and has *never* been accomplished in a movie.

2) A group of men are hidden in the hills of a western badlands watching something approaching below: a band of outlaws, Indians, cattle rustlers, posse—can't be sure. Their leader asks one of the group to get him the pair of binoculars from the knapsack so he can see more. The camera shot changes now to show the leader's face looking down into the valley, while behind him the guy he asked to help is shown moving away, only to return in a few seconds with the binoculars, which he gives to his leader, who takes it and surveys the scene below. The next film clip shows the scene as he sees it through high-powered binoculars, even including the unreal top and bottom semicircles so you know what he's looking through. You are given this close-up magnified view for several seconds, after which he moves these high-powered glasses to the right, then left, taking it all in. And you know what's amazing? *Never— not even once*—does the scene waver, nor do such scenes in *any* similar film. Nobody can hold binoculars and look through them for even two seconds without some form of manual shaking. What did he have, the first pair of nineteenth-century SteadyCam binoculars?

The Dodgers Should Have Listened To Grandpa

I loved my paternal grandfather, a sincerely religious good man of wisdom, high moral values, ethical standards and so much more. In addition, he possessed a roguish sense of humor.

Days earlier, the Brooklyn Dodgers had won a home game by a large score—something like 10 to 3; the next day they lost, 3 to 2. It was September; they were in a tight pennant race, and as a rabid fan the frustration of the second-day performance was still with me on Sunday, when the family got together. Grandpa was no fan of sports but was in the room when the subject came up, and he picked up on my aggravation. After a few seconds of silence he spoke, and we all listened alertly. "What they should have," he mused, "is a bank account. They win a game by seven runs, deposit six of them. When they lose a game by one run, withdraw two and add them to the total, so they win by a run. If they have any left over at the end of the season, leave them in the bank so next year they start out with some runs, and what they leave earns interest so the account has even more for them to use."

His deadpan expression made me think for a moment that he was serious, but his twinkling eyes betrayed mirth, so everyone smiled and moved on to another topic. Too bad, because maybe one of us should have gone to Ebbetts Field and given the idea to the team's management. Maybe they would have listened and even considered the idea. If they had, it might not have taken another seven or eight years for Dem Bums to win their first World Series.

We're Not Gourmet Chefs—Just Get A Knife

Unless someone's profession involves food preparation I don't understand the appeal of expensive utensils, pots and pans. When a family member or friend serves a memorable meal I'll bet it was cooked and carved without using a French Dutch oven, a designer skillet, a $200 carving knife or a computer-controller coffee maker.

We've had the pleasure of cooking for hundreds of guests over the years (we've even had a soups-only cookbook published) and I can assure you that not one has ever refused to eat his or her salad because each piece of diced celery wasn't precisely 13/97ths of an inch wide.

How The Use Of Electricity Became Common

The drone of murmuring in the smoke-filled room diminished at the sound of the Chairman's banging gavel. "Gentlemen, it's 1899, almost the 20th century. This Committee has been appointed solely to determine our nation's commercial, industrial and residential future with respect to electricity. Is it a threat or a blessing, and do we recommend banning or encouraging its use by everyone?" He paused momentarily. "Being unaffiliated with any political party and thus neutral, I shall only chair and monitor this meeting, which I now turn over to you." A man whose hand was raised stood up.

"Thank you, Mr. Chairman. I'm Tom Tillson, representing the Impulsives Party. Sir, we must allow everyone to benefit from this miracle, especially in large cities, where the smoke from burning candles every night has made the streets resemble foggy London. For the sake of safety as well as convenience, every city resident and farm dweller should have electricity and have it soon."

A heavy, cigar-smoking man rose, looked around and then began speaking slowly. "Bob Branford for the Cautionists or Cautionistas, as we're known in the North End. Sir, I don't think my colleague here realizes what he's inviting with respect to death, injury and destruction. Tom, how many adults in the parlor do you think will be blinded if they're sitting near a lamp when the bulb explodes, sending glass fragments into their eyes? How many more will be injured when they trip over the cord and maybe fall down the stairs? How many pets will be electrocuted when they chew through that cord? How many kids will be burned or even killed when they stick their fingers into a toaster in use or into an outlet while licking the wall? How many families will lose their lives and homes because of fires caused by too many devices using too much electricity?"

You could hear a pin drop; then, Tom Tillson responded. "Bob, of course, greatly exaggerates the situation to a point of ridiculosity. I'm certain any potential dangers will be minimized or eliminated by laws governing product design, manufacture, installation or use, and with typical government oversight, what can go wrong?"

That triggered a noise explosion, as passionate agreement with one view clashed with vehement opposition to the other. With the Chairman's gavel banging rapidly and authoritatively it was, in fact, rather exciting—one might even say electrifying. In the midst of all this tumult another man, well known to all, stood up.

"Reverend Gregory Gilcrest, Mr. Chairman, speaking on behalf of the Regressionists. I am troubled—yea, even dismayed—by the ease with which God's will is ignored or forgotten. True, the Lord commanded that there be light, and there was light, but then He also separated the light from the darkness, and saw that it was good. If the Lord had wanted constant light, surely He of infinite power was capable of causing it to be. This...this... electric passion is the work of the ungodly, the Devil's temptation. The Lord has spoken to me, and He decries—nay, deplores—such activities. It was His will that caused William McKinley to be our new President rather than his reckless opponent. I cannot force you to hearken unto God's will, but if this menace to society is approved, God forbid, I swear before Him that my congregants will either refuse to participate in this electric business or be expelled from both our faith and my church."

It was so quiet in the room that one could hear a floating smoke ring dissolve. A minute or so later another person got up to speak. "Harvey Hemple, Mr. Chairman, founder of the Hellwithits. I have great respect for Reverend Gilcrest, but this is not a religious issue; it's a matter of worldwide competition and progress. Given his line of reasoning Prometheus will spend eternity in hell for having given us the gift of fire. Without him the fire that destroyed Chicago 28 years ago would never have occurred, never mind all the others who have died at the stake by order of similar religious zealots. And what about the heathen who invented the wheel? How many of us will die in the next century in accidents involving stagecoaches or railroad passenger cars, not to mention these newfangled horseless carriages and trolley cars? Will many blacksmiths and canal boat companies be put out of business by these wheeled vehicles? Of course. Progress has a price, but just think of all the new jobs and opportunities this will create for our nation.

No, sir; electricity must be welcomed, and for those who can't afford it, the government must provide service to the poor at no cost—for free!"

Within seconds, the level of angry shouting and near-fisticuffs reached such a level of intensity that the Chairman had to end the meeting and schedule resumption for 10:00 AM the next morning. As the members slowly gathered up their papers, put on their coats, scarves and hats and began heading towards the exit, Bob Branford caught up with Tom Tillson and put his arm across Tom's shoulder. "A hell of a meeting, I must say. By the way, Tom, you expressed yourself quite well today, especially being new to this game; I did enjoy it. You made a good point, although it really doesn't matter."

Tom smiled. "Hello, Bob; good to see you again. Thank you for the compliment, but I must say your presentation was much more passionate than mine—good job. By the way, what did you mean when you said that I made a good point but it really didn't matter?"

Bob stopped, removed his arm from Tom's shoulder and turned to face him, looking him squarely in the eye. "Tom, even if this committee recommends expanding electric use what difference does it make? The nation just elected a new President, and McKinley's a Traditionalist! Do you really think he's going to let it happen?"

Tom frowned. "Well, unfortunately, you may be right; I guess I can't argue with what you're saying. Still, there is a chance..."

Bob started to laugh. "Oh, sure, there's always a chance. Just like there's always a chance that man will be able to fly to Europe some day. It may take another hundred years, if ever, to figure out how to do it, but I suppose it's always possible. Come on, Tom, be realistic, not idealistic. Do you really think McKinley's going to even give serious consideration to this electricity issue?"

"No, I don't," Tom responded, "but I wasn't thinking of him—I was thinking of the Vice-President, Teddy Roosevelt."

Bob regarded him with amused curiosity. "Him? You're joking. Do you really think McKinley or anyone in Washington is going to listen to that brash loud-mouthed hunter? Why do you think he was chosen to be Vice-President? We got tired of listening to his verbal crusades to help the poor—'the common man.' Christ, he began to sound like a goddamned Modernist. The only reason he was chosen to be Vice-President was to shut him up and get him out of the way so he couldn't do any harm, since we all know how important the job of Vice-President is—about as useful as tits on a bull."

Tom nodded. "True, but hey, you never know. Someday,..." Bob laughed. "What—he might be President? Teddy Roosevelt, President? Oh, yeah, right...that's really gonna happen!"

Perhaps One Of The Most Wonderful Means Of Transportation

One cannot help but be awed by structures remaining from long-lost civilizations with brilliant engineers who somehow produced everything from pyramids in Giza to Stonehenge on Salisbury Plain to whole communities carved into rock in Mesa Verde. Seeing or traversing these wonders leaves one with feelings of incredulity, disbelief and boundless admiration that such gems could be and actually were accomplished two, three, even five thousand years ago. But there is something else to be experienced: an emotional connection that comes when one can feel being part of something even older, perhaps timeless. For this, visit Russell Cave in Bridgeport, Alabama, which is literally in the upper northeast corner of the state. It's but one of many cave dwellings or rock shelters that provided housing for Paleolithic man, but Russell Cave itself was home to the native peoples known as the Paleo over *nine thousand* years ago.

Knowing that and keeping it in mind, imagine entering the cave by yourself or perhaps with one other person, and you're the only ones there. As your eyes adjust to the diminished light they sweep the area, revealing its relative enormity as well as traces along the ground of the life and activity that once existed here. Soon you spot some of the wall artwork, which you examine out of curiosity and fascination. Turning around and looking up provides a view of the ceiling, surprisingly much higher than you might have expected. Lowering your gaze you look outside at a beautiful scene of woods with a garden-like path, perfectly framed by the cave's opening. Standing there for a moment or two and letting your imagination breathe, you are caught up in the mystical aura of which you were cognizant before but which has now partnered with a sense of the dissolution of time that is virtually impossible to describe. You are seeing and hearing and sensing and feeling the environment from a completely different perspective, as though transported through time. For the moment, you have become a Paleo, and simply viewing or merely walking around a man-made masterpiece that's only a couple of thousand years old or so cannot even begin to approximate such a gratifying adventure.

You're A Grand Old Flag

My mother was listening to a song on the radio one day when I was a child; it was George M. Cohan's "You're a Grand Old Flag." After the orchestral introduction, the vocalist began:

> You're a grand old flag,
> You're a high-flying flag
> And forever in peace may you wave!…

Mom pursed her lips and shook her head from side to side during the third line, but then seemed to enjoy the rest of the performance. When the song ended, I asked her what was wrong with the song, or what she didn't like about it. She smiled.

"I love the song," she said. "I just think it's a shame they had to change the second line."

I had no idea what she was talking about. "What do you mean?"

Then she explained. "The original words were: 'You're a grand old flag, you're a high-flying *rag*,' not flag. He had to change 'rag' to 'flag' because he was talking about the American flag, and it was considered disrespectful to refer to it as a 'rag.' I just found that out recently. I had always wondered why a gifted songwriter like he was couldn't have come up with some other rhyming word to use to end the second line instead of repeating the word 'flag'."

I was impressed and still am, since even today most people don't know this. As for me, ever since that day I hear the words as "high-flying rag" in my mind whenever I hear Cohan's great song.

The Untold Story Of Creation

God created the heavens and the earth in six days, and saw that it was good. On the seventh day, in the midst of a well-deserved rest, He was evaluating His work and, looking down, saw Adam eating dinner in silence, disconsolate, with no emotional involvement, and realized that something basic but critical was missing in his life, which He determined to rectify.

Thus, on the eighth day, God created garlic.

Let's Get Back To Cell Phone Basics

Cell phones should be used only in a crisis. When someone calls her best friend in tears to announce that she's out of lipstick, that's not exactly an emergencical situation. A better example is when one is stuck in traffic, where a cell phone is needed that can perform just four simple functions:

1) Store up to a dozen important numbers
2) Transmit outgoing calls
3) Receive incoming calls

4) Contain a foolproof chamber with room to hold liquid and vaporize it at the press of a button.

After all, if one is stuck in traffic, isn't it more important to be able to use your cell phone to go to the bathroom than to watch pictures of some woman's underpants being taken on an escalator by someone with a cell phone camera?

How To Tell If You're Getting Fresh Fish

While visiting friends in Pittsburgh last May they took us to the city's famous Strip District, a venerable section well known for its delicious places to eat and exotic foods for sale from around the world. It's a fun place to be if you can stand friendly people, great cooking and just happen to be hungry. Dave and I walked along the sidewalk behind our wives as they looked into the windows of the stores on one side of the main street, occasionally entering one to look for specific specialties. Soon we all went into a store that had various types of fish packed in ice within display cases. I looked at some of them and, judging by the condition of the eyes and the lack of a strong fish smell, remarked that these seemed to be really fresh.

Dave nodded. "There's a fish store further down the block that has even fresher fish." I was impressed. "You're kidding; really? How do you know—I mean, how can you tell?" He smiled, and responded. "Because they're swimming around in tanks, and you can't get much fresher than that."

How Matzos Changed The World

Thousands of years ago in Egypt, after 400 years of being slave laborers, the Hebrews at last were allowed by the Pharaoh to leave, an event recorded in the Old Testament as the Exodus. Although forty years of wandering in the desert would follow, things started out well enough—that is, until the Pharaoh changed his mind and ordered his troops to go after and retrieve the newly-freed slaves.

Word of the impending peril reached the Hebrews as they were in the process of making bread. They had to act quickly, which left no time for the dough to rise and become a regular loaf. The result was a hitherto unimagined, totally new product: matzo.

A matzo is a thin square wafer of unleavened bread traditionally eaten by Jews at the Passover Seder, a celebratory commemoration of the Exodus. Measuring roughly seven inches per side, there are some 16 rows of perforations running from top to bottom across the surface, making it easier to break the matzo in half, in quarters or in pieces. It also makes an ideal cracker to use anytime as the basis for a variety of tempting hors d'œuvres, since it's made only from flour and water, with no added sodium or sugars to distort the taste of its topping. In addition, it makes a great snack topped with butter or some other spread, or just plain, which is pretty healthy. Perhaps these and other reasons explain why the popularity of matzos for everyday use is increasing among all peoples.

But matzo is more than just good food. It was probably the first product that could be consumed totally and be made inexpensively with no need to recycle, a concept not even imagined centuries ago.

Just think about it: if a matzo breaks in use, you have the basis for all those hors d'œuvres and snacks, or for soup crackers. Don't need the pieces for those things right now? Store them in a sealed container or plastic bag; they'll last indefinitely.

Ah, but what if matzos break during the manufacturing process? No problem; just crumble them more and you have the makings of a new product—farfel, a granular form of noodles. And should those pieces somehow get ground up too small you have matzo meal, the basis for matzo balls—those small, round dumplings that are so wonderful in soups. Never do you ever have to reprocess or toss away matzo, much less recycle. How cost-effective, efficient and environmentally friendly is that?

And yet these brilliant innovations remained either unknown or unappreciated throughout the world for an incredibly long time. It wasn't until about 1900 that these techniques were discovered and their potential fully understood. Global examples are many, but to give just one, Italians realized that they could adapt these ideas to produce multiple variations of their essential foods to meet their own needs. And thus the simplistic heart of basic Italian cuisine—spaghetti and tomato sauce—was able to expand beyond belief. Matzo became the model for lasagna; farfel became the precursor of the small pellet-like orzo, then the similar tubettini, pasta a riso, stellini and more. These led to larger and varied forms of noodles as well as shells, elbows, rotelli, rotini, ziti and literally dozens of other creative forms of pasta. The Italians then expanded the idea to include cooked tomato products: when whole peeled tomatoes became damaged they became diced tomatoes. If the dice became too small during processing, they were turned into crushed tomatoes or, if they shredded, they became purée. It wasn't long before the word "spaghetti" became synonymous with Italy, and their cuisine became wildly popular worldwide.

And all because of the humble matzo. (Hey, who knows? It might have happened this way.)

In Fact, Many Gourmet Specialties Were Created Accidentally (Or, A Pillar Of The Community)

Unhappy with the rising immorality in Sodom and Gomorrah, The Lord vowed to destroy them. However, hearkening to a plea from Abraham to spare the cities if ten good people could be found, God relented to the extent that the good people would be allowed to leave and travel safely to the hills, on condition that no one looked back. The exodus was proceeding well until Lot's wife couldn't contain her curiosity and turned around to see what was happening. Instantly, she was turned into a pillar of salt.

Of course, being Jewish, it had to be kosher salt...

Guys: Two Things To Consider When You Think You Might Be In Love

Actually, fellas, there are many factors that come into play, but these two really are important. The first is definitely more difficult.

1) Sometimes, stop and think with your brain, not your gonads.

2) Mentally test yourself and go with your gut, as follows:

Imagine that your girlfriend just now informed you that she has accepted a new job halfway across the nation that starts next month, so she'll be moving there in two weeks. What is your gut reaction, that instinctive feeling that you get before you can even formulate a thought? Is it nothing, just total indifference, as though you had just heard on the radio that pork-belly futures were higher on Wall Street? Worse yet, were you instantly overcome by an enormous sense of joy or relief, excited by the idea of again being free and available? Or were you struck by a sense of shock, upset, panic, confusion or loss, perhaps indicating how much she means to you, how important she has become in your life and how the possibility of losing her is unimaginable, unthinkable?

Don't dwell on it; just go with your gut. (Of course, if she fails to ask you to go with her, that tells you something, too, doesn't it?)

The Numbers Racket

The musical world has always been impressed by the fact that Ludwig van Beethoven composed nine symphonies, a number that seemed insurmountable. After all, Franz Schubert had also written only nine. Antonin Dvorák was credited with five until the late 20th century when musicologists found four more, which raised his total to the magic nine. Then, in 1909, Gustav Mahler composed his ninth symphony, and the musical world waited, hopeful, excited.

Mahler delivered; a year later he published his tenth symphony. Then Dimitri Shostakovich did even better: over the next several decades he composed 15 symphonies. How impressive is that?

Very—if the musical world continues to overlook the fact that a couple of centuries earlier Wolfgang Amadeus Mozart composed 41 symphonies and Franz Josef Haydn an astounding 104!

Actually, New York Is The Henpire State

It's a beautiful, variegated state that has every right to be known as "The Empire State." But I just can't help it—maybe it's only me, but if you look at an outline of New York State's boundaries, using just the slightest bit of imagination, isn't it easy to picture the outline of a young chick that is facing right, looking straight ahead?

Math Problems

"Math is the bane of his existence" was one of the accurate facts noted about me in my high school yearbook. I have no trouble with arithmetic (in fact I'm pretty good at it), but math is something else. Since I had no intention of becoming a scientist or a professor of mathematics, I had little patience with its basic abstract concepts. I could appreciate the beauty, even the excitement, of manipulating various challenging components to create an inventive solution, but this just wasn't for me—I was too practical. If I was lost in the woods and came to a river on the other side of which was a tall tree, I couldn't care less about determining the angle formed between the treetop and the point at which I was standing. My objective would be to follow the river and attempt to get the hell out of the woods.

Although I have no proclivity towards math, I think part of the blame for my ineptitude in complex or theoretical mathematics lies with the high school teachers. Not one ever so much as suggested to us disinterested sufferers that geometry, trigonometry or even algebra could be regarded as tools to expand the mind and its ability to think outside the box. To most of us they were just required subjects to be endured and passed, never to be used in real life. I might as well have taken courses to master the nuances and subtle differences between the southern and northern dialects of the Peloponnesian language.

Adding to this burden, of course, were the problems themselves. Looking at them as a student, but from a purely practical rather than a potentially educational point of view, three different types as presented come to mind.

The first is just downright annoying. If I ask someone, "How old is your sister?", either tell me it's none of my business or give me her age, but don't respond with "My sister is twice as old as our neighbor's dog, who was run over by a man who died one year before he would have been four times older than the car he was driving, which he purchased used from someone whose son is exactly my sister's age."

Then there was the "illustrative example" type. After learning a new skill—say, multiplication—a problem would be presented and solved that used that skill: well intended but deceptively simplistic. "A candy bar costs $1.00. Johnny wants to buy five candy bars. How much money does he need to buy the five candy bars?" The example would then show the use of multiplication in the solution:

$$\begin{array}{r} \$1.00 \\ \underline{\times\,5} \\ \$5.00 \end{array}$$

Simple enough, and they even gave the answer. Then, following the example, another problem would be given, this one to be solved by the learner—certainly an effective way to reinforce knowledge, or so it would seem. The trouble is, it began something like this:

"A multi-national corporate conglomerate with 17.6% of its total net profit derived from two products produced in six locations in Australia..." and proceeded to present a financial scenario so complicated that a team of the world's most perceptive accountants would have needed three weeks to figure it out.

Finally, there were the "obvious logic" problems: "'A' can beat 'B' in ping pong, and 'B' can beat 'C'; hence it follows that 'A' can beat 'C'" (transitive equation). Mathematically true, but in real life, "C" could beat "A", and often did. It's called "an upset victory."

But that's not what made logic problems so irritating; it was the unabashedly arrogant use of the hated word *hence* and others like it (*thus, obviously, of course, therefore* and *it goes without saying*), implying that only a moron could fail to understand and accept the unmistakably apparent conclusion. It was that demeaning verbiage that was such a put-off for me.

Now some mathematical educators might not agree, or think I'm being petty. Okay; to show that I can be open-minded, I'll accept that for the moment and present my last logical conclusion in their traditional manner. "Math teachers teach math; I'm having trouble learning math; hence it goes without saying, of course, that the only solution must therefore be obviously interpreted and expressed thusly: it has to be the teachers' fault."

Give Us This Day…

Usually, when we go out to dinner, a basket containing various forms of bread, rolls, crackers, breadsticks or a combination of such is included. By the end of the meal it is not uncommon to have some left, especially if we're with friends and the basket has been emptied, thus causing the server to bring more. At one time these leftovers were taken back into the kitchen, perhaps to be arranged in another basket for another table. Now, though, by law, this cannot be done; leftovers must be disposed of, thrown away like garbage.

With over a billion people worldwide going to bed hungry every night, I find it unconscionable to be part of such unnecessary and extravagant waste. And that's why, no matter who's with us or how fancy or trendy the restaurant is, we always ask our server for a container into which we put all those leftover baked goodies to take home. Breads and rolls can always be toasted, used for sandwiches and appetizers or, if they get hard in a day, as croutons in soups and salads. The same is true for crackers and breadsticks, which also make nice munchies. Using leftovers may not help the hungry, but at least we're not increasing their pain by being wasteful with our overabundance. And I feel better about that.

The Lady And The Baby-Changing Station

Last year at an airport a young lady pushing a stroller stopped at a ladies room with a baby-changing station, removed her child and went inside. Apparently the changing station wasn't working because a few minutes later she emerged, carrying the same fat ugly child she went in with.

Two Suggestions To Improve Your Scrapbook

It's great to be able to take many days, even weeks, to go on a trip or vacation, which usually includes seeing various places and attractions. If you're like me you enjoy taking pictures, which will become part of your personal collection of treasured memories. With that in mind, here are two suggestions for your trip that may prove beneficial and add to the enjoyment of your scrapbook:

1) Look for any free pamphlets, brochures, booklets or circulars that are pertinent to the area you're in. You can usually find them in racks at any motel or hotel, at a nearby welcome or information center and certainly at the well-visited attractions themselves. What you want to do is take a moment to browse through them and look for pictures, historical background information or any narrative descriptions of the area or its points of interest. If you find any, take two copies of each just in case one contains items you'd like to save but they're on both sides of one page. Why save them to begin with? To go through when you get home and have gotten all your developed photos back and are creating that scrapbook. I've found that such brochures often contain shots I couldn't take ("No Flash Photography!") or didn't have to because theirs were taken from a better perspective or provided a broader panorama, or were shot under better weather conditions. Just as important, if some of your photos don't come out, or the film is damaged or lost, you have backup. Add their pictures to yours, along with any related written material, and you have a greatly enhanced scrapbook.

2) Many travelers buy picture postcards to send to family and friends. You may not, but buy some anyway for the same reasons you've been collecting those brochures—backup and enhancement. Postcards in particular offer scenes that you probably can't get otherwise: an aerial view of Miami Beach; museum art; a 100-year-old shot of Boston; Times Square at night. Others present "regular" shots of the attraction you're at or going to, but perhaps taken at sunrise or sunset, or of such quality that you know it's better than you could capture on film yourself. Not only can they save you the cost of the film you'd have to shoot and have developed, but at prices typically running around three or four for a dollar they're worth it, especially given their great quality. You can usually find them in stores or the gift-shop part of various attractions or hotels.

Are People Becoming Too Internet-Dependent?

Recently, relatives who were getting rid of household items for which they no longer had any use gave us, among other things, an electric broiler and rotisserie. We transported the unit home, but it was a few days before we got to check it out and when we did, it turned out that the power cord that activates the heating coil was missing. A call to them and a search on their part yielded nothing.

Then I remembered that we had to go to Home Depot tomorrow, and they carry plugs. Rather than take and write down approximate measurements, why not bring the coil with us, show it to the person who would be helping us and get precisely the power cord we need?

Good thought, except that when we showed the coil to the two guys who were helping us, they both agreed that they had nothing even remotely like it. When I asked if they knew of anyone who might carry the cord we needed (even if it was a competitor), they were pretty sure nobody would because it was for that specific item. One of the guys, though, had an idea: why not go on-line to check out kitchen appliances or cookware? This triggered the other fellow to suggest that we browse, looking at images and searching for any that might resemble the unit we had brought in and if we found any, how to see them in greater detail or if not, how to obtain related information about food groups or cooking clubs, and so on.

We listened, nodding. Then I asked, "How will all this help us?" The first young man spoke up. "It may help you identify your unit or maybe even give you the name of the manufacturer."

At this point Barbara glanced down at the unit for a second, turned it over and quickly scanned it again, then looked along the side at the point where the coil's plug would have emerged, an area surrounded by a shiny engraved metal shield. Then she looked up.

"It's made by Farberware. It's their Model 450, 1500 watts, 115 volts," she announced, smiling.

They seemed stunned that she had obtained this information off-line, but agreed that we had what we needed. We thanked the two most sincerely for their help, which we did appreciate, and headed out to our car, thankful that we were probably among the last few thousand people in America that still were not on the Internet.

It's Time For Mileage

Long Island is a beautiful strip of land situated in the extreme southeastern corner of New York State. It's about 120 miles long, running east from New York City out to Montauk Point. Its width, however, varies from barely 10 miles to a maximum of 24, which doesn't leave much room in this densely populated part of the state for too many major roads. This becomes problematic, since most of its residents live here year-round and drive a lot, whether to work each day or to get elsewhere. Adding to these congestion woes are the island's beautiful resorts and beaches, some of which are among the finest in the world, attracting not only locals but tons of tourists.

Many of us visit Long Island infrequently, and if it's to visit new or relocated friends and family for the first time, we're not sure just how far out they live (after all, there are many towns within a 120-mile length).

So it seems normal, even natural, to ask them about how many miles they are from a particular point—say, after you cross the Throggs Neck Bridge. Invariably, the answer you'll get is "45 minutes" or some other figure of time, but *never* one in miles. You can ask again, even specifying your need to know mileage, but the answer will be the same. You can even point out that time is meaningless because you know about the roads, and 45 minutes at 20 miles an hour isn't the same as 45 minutes at 60 miles an hour, but it doesn't matter: Long Islanders just don't use or see the need for mileage, even when they move out. ("I used to live 20 minutes from Coney Island; now it takes an hour to drive to Disneyworld!")

Who created this useless form of navigational information, and how has it survived and why does it still exist?

The Eyes Of Texas Are Upon You

But for Alaska, which we'll visit soon, we've toured every state extensively—except Texas. It's not that the Lone Star State doesn't offer much to see and do; it's more about the overall attitude of its natives, which leaves us feeling uncomfortable at best and wary or apprehensive at worst. They present that collective smug, superior, arrogant "everything here is bigger and better than where you come from" face that makes you want to avoid, ignore or leave them.

Once, for instance, we drove into the state from Oklahoma and stopped at a welcome center. We picked up some Dallas brochures and asked if they had any litter bags, explaining that we had run out because we really do use them. The woman, saying nothing, gave us one small one. We thanked her, and I unfolded it and looked at the front; as expected, there was a message printed on it.

Now you would think that it would be something appreciative or at least polite, like you'd find on such bags in other states: "Thank you for keeping our state clean" or "Please don't litter." This one, however, presented a blunt warning: "Don't Mess With Texas." I looked up at the woman, resisting the urge to say something nasty, and instead just commented "Well, uhhmm, that's interesting." She smiled and responded: "Well, you're in Texas now."

I could relate other personal and more serious examples, but I'll pass on that; you get the idea. More important, we know we're not alone in our reluctance to go back to Texas—far from it. Many people we've known over the years feel the same way about Texans in general. What we can't exactly figure out is what makes them that way or how they got to be that way.

Recently we were discussing an issue with friends. To illustrate a point I was trying to make, I concluded with, "You know, like the Texas attitude towards anyone else." Both understood, having gone through similar experiences there. After trading horror stories I asked, "Has anyone figured out what makes them that way?" Wendy thought about it for a few seconds, then began to respond. "I think," she said slowly, thoughtfully, "that someone extracted the worst traits and characteristics from people in the nation, combined them, then put them through a process to condense them and make them stronger, more intense—you know, like making concentrated orange juice—and used the result to create Texans."

Attention Deficit Disorder? You're Kidding!

Isn't it amazing how youngsters who can't pay attention or concentrate on a subject for more than a few seconds can not only learn and memorize the lyrics to dozens of rap, rhythm and blues or rock numbers but also perfectly mimic every vocal inflection and subtle dance nuance as presented by the performers?

Weissman's Laws Of Driving On Two-Lane Roads

You're driving on a two-lane country road with a fixed speed limit—let's say 55 miles per hour. The direction in which you're traveling doesn't matter; what does is whether or not you're the sole vehicle in that lane. If you are, fine; but if you're not, one of these two laws applies almost invariably:
1) If you are the lead vehicle, you could be going 65 miles an hour, and the driver behind you will be climbing up your rear end either trying to pass you or to get you to speed up.
2) If you're behind the lead vehicle, that driver will be going no more than 45 miles an hour.

Why Pick On Chauvin, Of All People?

There is nothing wrong with females being annoyed, even upset with men who unfairly or excessively belittle them. Of course they want to lash out and get back at these guys, and understandably so. But there are some things these ladies should consider—for one thing, the key word: *unfairly*. If a man says that it seems to him there are more professional male chefs than female, don't jump all over him and accuse him of being anti-female. He's just expressing his opinion, which might be based on watching TV cooking shows, personal observations in restaurants or an article he read in a paper; in addition, he may be right. When I'm driving and see a car on the soft shoulder with a flat tire being changed, it's always a guy doing it; if there's a woman present, she's standing by with arms folded across her chest, watching either him or traffic going by. If I make my usual "Why can't *she* change it?" comment, that's no reason to go on a verbal male-bashing binge or call me a male chauvinist pig; save the righteous indignation for really deserving situations.

And that's another thing: why pick on Chauvin? He was just a French soldier who was an excessive patriot and Napoleon devotée. His fame lay in being overly supportive *of* issues, not against them. He might have been a rabid supporter of adopting dogs, but that doesn't mean he lambasted cats or people who preferred them.

I'm certain women will reconsider and perhaps attack men more tactfully, but if not, aren't they just female chauvinist sows?

American Cooking Is The Best

Every country produces imaginative, delicious, even exotic food masterpieces that result in great dining experiences. Perhaps France is the first country that comes to mind in such conversations, and with good reason; many of their dishes are exquisite and inimitable.

But maybe that's because they have to cook that way.

Leo was a U.S. Army soldier in Europe during World War II who lived in Paris for a couple of years after the war ended. I found this out when we worked together on a project in New Jersey, and was always fascinated by his lunchtime war stories and experiences. One day I happened to mention that my wife had prepared coq au vin for dinner the previous evening. His smile was replaced at once by a puzzled look and he asked, "Why?"

Caught by surprise, I stammered, "Be-because, uh, we…like it."

It took a second or so, but the look on his face changed to one of disbelief, then acceptance. "Oh," he said, quietly.

I was curious. "Why? What's wrong with coq au vin?"

"Oh, nothing," he explained. "If you like it, that's fine; I was just surprised that you would even bother making it when you can get good poultry here in the U.S."

Anyone can kill and skin something that moves, smother it in some kind of sauce or gravy and cook it, but for simple, honest, down-to-earth wholesome hearty food that pretty much has to stand on its own, you just can't beat good old solid United States cooking.

Fred Weissman

Rethinking Common Sense And Sanity

If you had told people in the early 1960s that you were carrying a recording of all nine Beethoven symphonies in one of your jacket pockets, the complete Encyclopædia Britannica in your other jacket pocket, four complete Hitchcock movies in your shirt pocket, and in one of your pants pockets a cordless telephone that could also take still or moving pictures without film and transmit them instantly to anywhere in the world, how long do you think it would have taken before you were either locked up in jail or delivered outright to Bellevue as a precaution for being an obvious menace to society?

Chapter 11 –

Check Out These Briefs

1) The most effective way to cut down on gas emissions? When that guy says, "Pull my finger!", don't.

2) We should all be far more concerned with the religious or political extremism of some people than by the sexual orientation of others.

3) There is a three-syllable word that practically pronounces itself when spelled rapidly, with emphasis on the second half of each syllable; the word is "potato." Try spelling it aloud as described, and practicing it: "pYO-tYAE-tYO." It may not strike you as amusing, but at least it's useless.

4) Drink to me only with thine eyes and I'll be happy to pick up your bar tab anytime we go out!

5) With so many cooking shows on television I'm still waiting for one episode in which the chef, who's been "ahhh"-ing or "mmmm"-ing throughout every step of its preparation, finally finishes the dish, tastes it and blurts out, "Oh, my God! This tastes like shit!"

6) With hundreds of TV channels, radio stations, newspapers, magazines and billboards nationwide, how much does constant advertising add to the price of products we buy?

7) Much of the world may hate the United States, but when's the last time you saw waves of Americans emigrating to any other country in search of a better life? (about 1965)

8) Richard Wagner's opera *"Die Meistersinger"* contains a choral

number entitled "Wach' auf!" Believe it or not, I was past 40 before I learned that it wasn't a way of telling someone in German to either get lost or go masturbate.

9) Come to think of it, I was in my fifties before I found out that an expectorant was not a pregnant woman.

10) Many worthwhile charities sponsor "walks" nationwide to raise money for their cause or promote awareness of it. We've all probably seen hundreds of men participating in walks for breast cancer and ovarian cancer, but when was the last time you saw a woman walk for prostate cancer?

11) If I may, I'd like to wax poetic for a moment: Madame Tussaud, a good place to go.

12) Within the past few months, at least five Catholic churches in lower New York State have been closed down by the archdiocese. Is this the start of mass extinction?

13) Czech composer Zdenek Fibich (1850-1900) wrote several classical music selections. Although virtually unknown today, he could have assured that he would not be forgotten by simply naming his firstborn child Sunna.

14) We all hope that medical research will eventually cure, eliminate and someday prevent cancer and other life-threatening illnesses, to which we are all vulnerable. If acting in the best interest of this nation is the purpose of government, how much more quickly could this goal be reached if Congress allocated just 1 minute of spending each day to this worthwhile cause?

15) *We are all much older now than we were when we were young.*
    —Testicles (387-314 B.C.E.)

16) "Live each day as though it were your last" is a foolish and pessimistic way to approach life. One would be spending every day in church praying or saying goodbye to family, or further maxing out credit cards in unimagined indulgences. I much prefer "There's always tomorrow."

17) In today's whacked-out world, the apple doesn't fall very far from the oak tree.

18) Isn't it strange that physiological conditions exclusive to females get names such as *men*struation and *men*opause?

19) One of the funniest oxymorons ever: an English chef.

20) A prostitute who sells herself and her services for personal gain affects only herself and maybe one other person. A politician who does the same thing can affect the entire nation. When it comes to going after criminals, let's get our priorities straight.

21) These days, the only way a man can wind up on top in an encounter with a woman is to assume the missionary position when making love.

22) My two favorite four-letter "f" words: "food" and "free."

23) A cook who can prepare good food is more impressive than a chef who can crack open eggs using only one hand.

24) If a person is functional enough to realize and admit that he's dysfunctional, which is he?

25) Is it true that Bugs Bunny died from a carroted artery?

26) If Europeans are so adept at technological innovation, how come they still can only produce toilet paper that feels either like crêpe paper or Sight Savers?

27) Diarrhea *(n):* Emergency evacuation.

28) Trendy places are merely establishments where the effete meet the élite.

29) I know many people from China, Japan and Korea, all of whom are perfectly content being themselves, know who they are and where they are headed. I assume this means they never have to worry about becoming disoriented.

30) My newest (and perhaps saddest) original oxymoron: an "ethical politician."

31) When I want to get my wife's attention or have something to say to her, I typically begin with "Oh, sweetie" or some similar phrase, such as "Oh, by the way, darling" or "Hey, love." Women think that's just wonderful and gush over it ("Oh, that is *so* sweet!" "Isn't that lovely?"). Well, I certainly adore my wife, but to tell you the truth, at my age, who the heck can remember her name?

32) Many African Americans were slaves in the U.S. for some 250 years, and a lot of their descendants feel that entitles them to government compensation. Well, many of my Hebrew ancestors were slaves in Egypt for about 400 years; how much does the Egyptian government owe me?

33) If men and women are equal, how come males can simply walk into a men's room in a public place while females typically have to join a waiting line for the same purpose?

34) I picked up a package of chicken leg quarters the other day at our local supermarket. The label boasted "No Artificial Ingredients." I was skeptical, but checked each leg in the package back home, and they were telling the truth: there was not one plastic limb.

35) To me, the word "stewardess" evoked an image of a busy lady caring totally for her airborne passengers, but now that she's a "flight

attendant" I can only picture someone in the restrooms restocking paper towels and toilet paper.

36) Mince – The one word in a recipe I hate to encounter when having to prepare certain raw vegetables.

37) Panus Angelicus – What my wife Barbara uses to make her heavenly jams and jellies.

38) Barbara's not Catholic, but having to put up with me for all these years certainly qualifies her for sainthood, as far as I'm concerned.

39) There was a TV car commercial guaranteeing no interest for two years, but that was not quite accurate. I saw that ad five years ago and I'm still not interested.

40) A couple recently bought a 35-year-old home and became its seventh owners, so why was yet another expensive full deed check and land survey required when the last ones were done barely two years ago?

41) Gay men use male public facilities like restrooms, saunas and showers, which could be a turn-on. I'm straight; why can't I at least use the ladies' room, for starters?

42) Come to think of it, anytime I take a shower, it's a turn-on.

43) When someone asks how a particular word is spelled and is told, "Look it up in the dictionary," how helpful is that?

44) Seeing a preserved or restored historic site is, for me, so much more meaningful than simply reading a plaque that begins "On this site once stood…"

45) Last week I found out that my net worth finally reached seven figures: $12,459.68.

46) Some people don't eat red meat; that's fine. But if you're one of them, and we ever invite you over for dinner, I'd have to know what color you'd like it painted instead.

47) The best restaurants almost always turn out to be the ones encountered by chance, usually on a last-minute "Why don't we try this place?" basis; rarely are they the pricey, inconsistent ones gushed over in trendy publications.

48) Time passes so quickly. I last showered just over a month ago, yet it seems like only last week.

49) That reminds me: next year is an even-numbered year—my favorite. That's when I not only get to use the bathtub but also to change the water *and* start a new bar of soap!

50) I can't recall the name of the last movie I saw in a theatre, but I remember that Charlie Chaplin got the girl.

51) Don't you feel sorry for those people who grumble about high gasoline prices while sipping their bottled waters?

52) 100 years ago people enjoyed recorded music on one-sided 78 rpm phonograph records called discs; today they listen to one-sided CDs called discs. We've come full circle.

53) Being found "Not Guilty" of charges doesn't necessarily mean that that person is innocent—just not found guilty.

54) So-called "Armchair Liberals" are élitists who are blindly and passionately defensive of African-Americans under all circumstances but wouldn't be caught dead living next door to one. I refer to them as "On-Paper Liberals" and wouldn't be caught dead living next door to one.

55) Can even a renowned world-class French chef ever create "Fleas Provençal" from scratch?

56) Any time we hear the town fire alarm go off, my wife and I each have the same prayer in our hearts: please, Lord, let all survive and let the damage be minimal.

57) Countless campaign buttons have been created for office-seekers, but to me the strangest one was a 1952 button for the Democratic Presidential candidate Stevenson and his Vice-Presidential running mate Kefauver, containing only their first names. The pin read "Adlai and Estes."

58) Making hard-boiled eggs, that's easy; peeling them? Well, that's something else. Maybe freshness matters, but I can tell you this: I've tried at least half a dozen recommended methods using all kinds of eggs, and not one has ever worked. Does anybody have any other suggestions?

59) Any given product may be twice as good as its counterpart, but does that make it worth four times the price?

60) Does anyone still use phrases like "unbeknownst to me"?

61) How is it that in today's politically correct world, when a woman is killed, the term "manslaughter" is still used?

62) I've said it for years and I stand by it: when something goes wrong, it's always a woman. Yes, I know that's not always true, and feminists might find it offensive, but I don't recall the French advising "Cherchez l'homme."

63) Mutual admiration – When a wedding is scheduled to which you hope they won't invite you and they hope you won't attend.

64) Can't afford college? Get a day job and go at night! Do you think I got my Bachelor's Degree *and* my Master's Degree at night because I freckled in daylight?

Chapter 12 –

You Can't Make Up Stories Like These

The Day I Shot My Teacher

He not only wrote a daily public relations column for *The New York Times* but taught the subject at Fairleigh Dickinson University at night. Carl Spielvogel, in my opinion, excelled in both areas, and as a night student in my final year of study towards a Bachelor's degree I was fortunate enough to be a student in his class. A master of practicality, he challenged us with a few intriguing assignments during the fall semester, each daring us to invent an imaginative solution to a problem created to reinforce a newly-learned concept or give us experience in a basic area of public relations. The next week, some of us could volunteer or be selected to present our answers to the rest of the class, which would then judge them for effectiveness and worth and explain why they applauded or rejected the solutions. Being me, of course, I always tried to respond to the weekly challenges in as unorthodox a manner as possible.

The first assignment seemed simple enough: without using any profanity, vulgarities or questionable verbiage or actions, introduce yourself to the group in such a way that they will remember at least your last name at the end of class (and, presumably, the semester).

The following week a few students introduced themselves to us in the usual and expected associative manner, to wit: "My name is Bob Steeple, like you'd find on a church. When you think of my name, think of a church."

At the end of the evening, most of the rest of us in class remembered him as "Bob Church." Several more used the same approach. Then it was my turn.

I had decided to select a few examples of outstanding excellence of achievement in various fields and then assure the class that I could have surpassed those accomplishments: "'Venus de Milo' is one of the most beautiful examples of sculpture ever created, but it has no arms. From now on, whenever you see that statue, you're going to look at it and think, 'He did a great job, but Weissman could have done it better.'" I gave another two similarly outrageous but humorously-intended examples, then concluded: "This course is going to be one of the best any of us could ever take, because Mr. Spielvogel is a really terrific instructor. When it's finished, though, you're going to look back and reminisce, and you're going to think, 'He did a great job, but...'" I paused. The entire class helped me complete the sentence: "Weissman could have done it better!"

It was far more effective than merely urging everyone to think of me as "Weissman the Iceman." Believe me, at the end of class, everyone remembered my name—including Mr. Spielvogel, who all of us could sense was not exactly enthralled by my presentation.

There were other such challenges, but another noteworthy one I recall required us to create something to be affiliated uniquely with Pfizer Chemical Company. Most submissions were slogans, like Packard's "Ask the Man Who Owns One." Other entries included images in the style of the "Sun Maid Raisins" girl or "Uncle Ben." I submitted a cartoon character I dubbed "Liza, the Pfizer Chicken," wearing a sleeveless T-shirt with "Pfizer" across the front, whose *raison d'être* was to act as spokeschicken for the company. Most of the class liked it and, in fact, inquired about her health and well-being for the rest of the school year, always using her full name.

At the end of the last fall session, as we were leaving the room, Mr. Spielvogel asked each of us what we thought our grade should be. When my turn came I unhesitatingly answered "an 'A'," which seemed to surprise him, so I elaborated. "I know my solutions may not have pleased you, like the one to get the class to remember my name, but nothing I said was vulgar or disrespectful. It was meant to be original and funny and it worked, along with Liza the Pfizer Chicken. Everyone still knows my name and they know Liza, so I did meet the objectives of each assignment."

He listened, nodding, and when I was through he said, "Well, all right; thank you. See you next semester." I thanked him and left.

He gave me a "B"; still, I looked forward to the spring semester and a continuation of creative classes. I was not disappointed. The assignments were as challenging as ever and, for me, just as much fun. I must admit, though, that I did have mixed feelings on two or three occasions when Mr. Spielvogel gave us our new assignments and implored the class in a humorous manner to come up with good solutions "rather than those like Mr. Weissman has been sharing with us all year," or words to that effect. However, the weeks did pass smoothly and quickly, and soon the hanging weeping willow branches had light green leaves, temperatures had moderated, the aroma of spring filled the air and it wasn't getting dark until well after 8:00 PM. It was mid-May; the school term was almost over.

I was walking along the concrete path towards the building that housed the classroom when I was startled by noises coming from the shrubbery to my left: "Pssst…pssst…Fred." I looked, and was just able to make out the figure of a person. "Over here." I moved towards the urgent whispering and was soon facing the caller.

It was Mr. Spielvogel.

We exchanged greetings, then he spoke softly. "I could use your help tonight in a demonstration that will become the basis for the last assignment. It needs two people, and I think you'll like it. Will you work with me?" When I said "Sure," he smiled. "Good; thanks." With that he reached into his briefcase and pulled out a gun.

I froze. "Here; take it." Blurry images raced through my mind as his hand moved closer to mine. I took it and looked at it. "What am I to do with this?" He smiled, again. "I want you to aim it at me in class and pull the trigger." I was lost. "Wait a minute," I said, still a bit shaky. "You want me to shoot you? Look, we may not have a great relationship, but I never wanted to kill you. If you want to end your life, why choose me to do it? I mean, why not do it yourself?" He laughed quietly and responded. "Don't worry, you're not going to kill me; they're blanks." I opened the chamber and looked at the pellets, removed one and checked it. He was telling the truth. "Let me tell you what I'm planning. Perhaps the most important aspect of any kind of newspaper reporting is accuracy, and tonight's presentation is going to test that. I've asked you to do this because I think the class feels there's a certain amount of tension between us—which I hope isn't so—but that's exactly what makes you the most credible person I can ask to do this, and I think you'll have fun."

One more question remained. "How is this going to work?" He proceeded to explain. "I'll be talking to the class and explaining a few things, and I'll taunt you a couple of times—you'll recognize it. At that point, just take out the gun and shoot me. Say anything you want along with it, but no cursing. How about it? Sound good?"

It was intriguing. "Okay," I said, burying the cold barrel of the gun in the left side of my pants but leaving the handle accessible, covered by my suit jacket. Spielvogel checked his watch. "Ready to try this?" I nodded, lightly excited. "Okay," he said. "Let's go." When we reached the building I let him enter first and proceed. A minute later I followed, got to class and took my front-row seat.

And waited.

Nothing unusual or provocative happened during the first hour or so. As usual, he chose a few students to present their solutions to the prior week's problem, then elaborated on some points in our textbook. I was starting to get a little nervous, but I couldn't fidget too much because I didn't want to expose the gun handle or, worse yet, poke myself in the *cohones* with the long barrel. I looked at my watch; we had less than 30 minutes before the session ended.

And that's when it started.

Spielvogel was seeking suggestions about an aspect of product publicity, eliciting comments from the class. A few students who had raised their hands were selected (except me), and after hearing from them he opined that all were good examples, "far better than what Weissman would have come up with." They looked at me; I just sat, unmoving, and let him proceed. It didn't take much longer before he alluded to another one of my problem solutions in a negative manner. This time I mumbled something unintelligible and gave him an annoyed look, but still did nothing.

He concluded the topic by urging everyone to be original and creative but also to think before coming up with something "as laughable or ridiculous as 'Liza the Pfizer Chicken'." At that point I said, "That's it!" and began to stand up. "That's the third time tonight I've taken this crap. Enough is enough." I reached across my waist with my right hand, pulled out the gun, aimed it at him and pulled the trigger three times.

Some of the students, seeing the pistol, ducked or froze in their seats. A few stood up and moved carefully to the back of the room, crouching, but the expected explosion of sound from bullets being fired never happened. The gun simply clicked three times, after which I looked questioningly at it, then at Spielvogel and said, in a very sheepish voice, "Click...click...click?" He walked to where I was standing. "Sorry," I said, apologetically. "I don't know why it didn't work, or what went wrong. I didn't do anything. I'm really sorry." He smiled as he took the gun from me. "It's O.K.; you did a good job; thanks." He returned to his desk and faced the class. "You saw what just occurred here. I want you to write a newspaper article now. Describe what happened, and hand it in tonight." He put away the gun, glanced my way and thanked me again for my help. I sat, watching the class return to their seats and begin. Some wrote at a furious pace while others chose a pattern: pen a few words, pause, look up, think, then repeat the cycle. When everyone was finished and all papers had been submitted, Spielvogel wished all of us a good week and, with that, the session ended.

That next week was the last class of the semester, and it was a lively group that awaited the instructor's arrival. A couple of the guys began by coming over to me and asking who had cooked up last week's shooting bit. Others, too, had questions and comments. One lady was afraid that once I shot Mr. Spielvogel I'd continue shooting at them all, at random. Then an older man spoke. "I was a Marine. I can laugh now, but when I saw that gun come out, I dove instinctively for the floor and put my head under the chair. You really scared the crap out of me, but I'll tell you, you did a damned good job." Others agreed, and I thanked them. At that moment Mr. Spielvogel entered, greeted us and hoped we had recovered from last week's shenanigans. Then he explained why it was done.

The purpose of the shooting had been to illustrate how hard it could be to report an incident with complete accuracy, even if the writer had witnessed it. Only one student got it totally right, even to the inclusion of the three "click" comments when the gun misfired. Everyone else wrote the same story: a student pulled a gun, aimed it at the teacher and shot him. That one student was asked to read his paper, and he did, to warm applause. Spielvogel had made his point with stunning effectiveness, which is why he was so good.

At the end, as we were leaving the room, Mr. Spielvogel again asked each of us what we thought our grade should be. When my turn came I answered, "Truthfully, I think only a 'B'." He nodded.

He gave me an "A."

Sally

She was my best friend, and my closest. Since she was about seven months older, I was like her little brother. Sally and I were together almost every day, whether going for walks, playing games or just talking. I understand we even bathed together a few times, but I don't remember that. After all, I was only three years old.

We lived at the time in the Sheepshead Bay section of Brooklyn, New York, minutes away by car from Brighton Beach and Coney Island. Though we were to move to Manhattan two years later and never return as residents, my heart always swelled with love and longing whenever those halcyon days came to mind. I never forgot Brooklyn, and I never forgot Sally.

The next six years were happy and adventurous for me. It would require a novella to detail the many wonderful reasons why, but I'll just note here that these exciting years encompassed World War II and the start of the post-war exodus by many New Yorkers to various suburbs, including us to Teaneck, New Jersey. That turned out to be an event that severely altered my life, burdening me with a change in lifestyle and culture to which I never completely adapted and certainly never accepted. Fortunately, Teaneck was within 10 miles of the city and had the buses to get me there occasionally, which was very helpful over the next few years. But then, as work and night college created additional stress, what really helped was obtaining my driver's license. Now at least I could see friends and family more readily and escape to other parts of both states. Life in New Jersey was slowly becoming more bearable, but not quickly enough to diminish my longing to keep returning to the city.

Especially Brooklyn.

Having relatives there that I enjoyed seeing gave me the needed excuse for occasional visits, usually unannounced. I'd arrive early on a Sunday afternoon, which usually worked if they were home, spend a couple of hours or so with them, then head back. It was enough to keep me going for a few weeks. But on one Sunday something different occurred: my relatives were home but had to go out for a couple of hours. Did I want to come back? Sure, I said.

They left, and since it was such a beautiful spring day I decided to take a walk through this part of my favorite area of my favorite borough. I looked up and down the beautiful tree-lined street but suddenly felt compelled to head to my right, towards where I used to live, which I suddenly realized was not that far away—a bit over a mile, maybe. I decided to do it. It would be my first time back in 13 years! The anticipation filled me with excitement and happiness that lasted until I was almost there, when a strange sort of longing, almost homesickness, became dominant, and I knew why.

Somehow, I felt I had to try to see Sally.

Crazy. I wasn't even sure exactly which house out of several she lived in, although I had a rough idea. And even if I found her, come on—the last time we saw each other we were five years old, and now we were both 18. She certainly wouldn't recognize me, but what were the chances that she'd even remember me? Worse yet, what if her family had moved?

I was at the corner of the block on which I had once lived. The lovely playground was still there, adjacent to the brick building that had housed us in a bright, sunlit first-floor apartment with windows providing a view of the park. I looked up the street; nothing had changed. I walked past the park and the apartments, looking at the clustered, almost attached houses just beyond. The one I needed to find had to be among the first dozen or so. I continued to walk and look—not those two, or that one; not that one either, or that one...

Then I saw a pair of houses and I knew: one of them was hers.

I wasn't sure which one it was, so I selected the one on the right and rang the bell. A lady answered the door and smiled. "Yes?", she inquired. I returned the smile. "Hi. I'm looking for Sally. Is she here, by chance?" The lady shook her head. "Sally doesn't live here," she said. My heart sank, but her smile broadened. "She lives next door." I thanked her profusely, waited until she closed the door, moved to my left, took a deep breath and rang the bell. It took awhile but then the door opened and a beautiful, smiling young woman appeared, looking at me. "Sally?", I inquired, hesitantly. Her lovely face tilted slightly to the right, then her smile broadened and her eyes widened. "Little brother? Come on in!"

I couldn't believe this was really happening, but it was. I know we talked, probably updating each other on the last 13 years but, truthfully, I just remember looking at her and listening to her, then telling her after what seemed like only a few minutes that I had to be on my way but promising to see her again. That would be nice, she said. I kissed her on the cheek and left, euphoric.

We got together a few times over the next two years, always at her place. We'd chat for awhile, then go for a drive to the beach or another neighborhood and come back. They weren't dates, really, as much as opportunities for me to just be with her in my world—a loving, platonic friendship that I needed and she gave me.

One day, back home, I bumped into Joyce, an acquaintance who lived about three blocks away. When I asked her how things were going she said she had two items to share: first, she was pretty sure that she would soon be engaged to the nice guy she had been seeing for awhile, and second, she had gotten a promotion at work. When I asked her about her job it turned out she worked in Manhattan, not far from where I was going to be on Thursday anyway. I decided to add a surprise visit: pop in on her around lunchtime, chat for a few minutes, see her office and continue on my way.

When I got off the elevator that day I looked around and spotted the name of her company on one of the doors. I entered and went up to the receptionist, told her I was a friend of Joyce's who was in the area and had just dropped by to say hi. The woman paged her, spoke with her, then assured me she'd be out soon. I thanked her and waited, looking at an area filled with active people, interesting to observe and very helpful in making time pass as I continued to wait. Finally, I heard a familiar voice behind me. "Little brother! Is that you?" I turned around and looked. It was Sally.

I had never been a believer in fate or destiny, but this, along with our reunion in Brooklyn after 13 years, almost changed that. When Joyce finally appeared and seemed somewhat surprised to see a co-worker and I hugging I introduced her to Sally, explained who she was and swore that I'd had no idea she also worked here. I think she believed me because we talked for a few minutes and I did get to see her office.

A few weeks later I called our rabbi to set up a time to return a book of his that I had borrowed a few days earlier. Any time today would be fine, he assured me, and since I had to go to town anyway, I told him I'd be over soon. When I arrived he invited me to come on in and stay for a few minutes. His wife was already on her way into the kitchen to get some iced tea, so we sat down in the living room across from his widowed mother, who had been living with them for years. When he asked how things were going, I thought he'd get a kick out of my telling him about my recent experience at Joyce's office. He did enjoy it, then asked where I'd met "this other girl you've known for years" (I had not used Sally's name). When I said Brooklyn, where I'd lived as a child, his mom looked up from her needlework and asked where in Brooklyn. I mentioned the area, but she wanted more specifics. When I gave her the intersecting street and avenue she asked what the girl's name was. I responded with "Sally." She smiled and nodded. "I knew Sally; a lovely girl. She had a younger sister; they were nice children." It turns out she and her husband had lived further up the block, on the other side.

There is one other strange but related happenstance that occurred decades later that I'd like to share with you, if I may. The chorale in which my wife Barbara sang needed a new director at one point and was auditioning candidates. This interested me, so I was with her on a night when one particular lady was trying out. I thought she was really good, and when she finished I told her so. She was appreciative, and we talked a bit. I asked what she did; it turned out she taught school and also directed a chorus, both in Brooklyn. Of course, I had to tell her I had lived there as a child and when she asked where I told her exactly. She looked at me, shaking her head. "You're kidding! My father was the landlord of that building and I had an apartment there for a while, probably after you moved!"

Now at this point you may be wondering why Sally and I never married or at least "got involved." Well, I actually considered it but I think we sort of both knew that this could never turn into a serious relationship for many reasons, the most critical being our religious differences. I did see her over the next couple of years but even less frequently. Gradually, other demands and activities took over both our lives, and we lost contact. We never saw each other again.

And that, apparently, was the way things were destined to be.

The Cuddebackville Chronicles

Many people tell stories about traveling and meeting strangers who, it turns out, either live in their area (or used to) or have been there. It's always fun to hear these tales, but what surprises me is why the teller typically considers it so unusual and is almost always amazed that it even happened. To give a typical example:

"…and guess what? It turns out this guy's also from California! He lives in Beverly Hills and I live just a few miles away, in Santa Monica. He flew out of LAX the day before I did and where do we meet? Halfway across the world, in Hong Kong, of all places. Can you believe it? I mean, is that incredible, or what? And not only that—are you ready for this? We both love going to dinner at this fabulous Mexican restaurant on Sunset Boulevard in Hollywood. It's our favorite. Boy, talk about a small world!"

Nice story, but there's nothing remarkable about living in any crowded urban area or densely-populated suburb and bumping into someone from your vicinity when on a business trip or attending a conference or on a "guided tour" vacation. What's more unlikely is living in a rural area and encountering a person familiar with it—a place such as Cuddebackville, for instance, where we live.

It's not even a village, it's a hamlet—one of seven that comprise a town whose total population is less than 10,000. It's only about 75 miles from New York City, yet few beyond that range have ever heard of it or have any idea where it is, even when we describe nearby landmarks. That's why we're always surprised when once in a while someone recognizes the name and knows its location. Here are just a few of those instances that I think you might enjoy:

Barbara and I were vacationing in Virginia one year, visiting a few sites memorializing some of the major battles of the Civil War. We had just entered the Fredericksburg Battlefield Visitor's Center and were greeted by a pleasant gentleman behind a counter. After giving us brochures and mapping out a good route to follow if we were taking a walking tour of the grounds he asked where we were from. I said that we were from lower New York State, around Port Jervis. He nodded. "I used to date a woman from Cuddebackville." He told us her name. "She lived on the other side of the Neversink River, off _____ Road." Turns out we didn't know the woman, but then he remembered something else from two or three weeks ago. He went to the guest sign-in register and scanned for names from around that time, working his way backwards until he found what he was looking for, pointed to it and said triumphantly, "There; look at that!" Almost a month earlier, another Cuddebackville resident had visited, and this time his name was familiar.

We were at the University of Colorado in Boulder one year for "Odyssey of the Mind" World Finals, the conclusion of a creative annual program for youngsters in which both Barbara and I serve as judges. I was asked to be one of two "off-stage" judges who find the next few teams scheduled to perform, get them to a pre-staging area to check props, paperwork and other requirements, and try to ease their tensions with humor and encouragement.

The teams and their equipment wait in one of two areas, each the size of two gyms and reminiscent of a refugee displacement camp. On one search I threaded my way through the teams, looking for one from Pennsylvania that I finally found. When I asked where in the state they were from and they told me, I said I knew their town because I lived less than an hour away, on the other side of Port Jervis. At that point their head coach, who had been checking some forms, looked up and studied me for a few seconds. "Do you live in Cuddebackville, on _____ Road?" When I got over my surprise and said yes he identified himself and explained. "I used to live up the road, but we moved just around the time you were moving in. I saw you working outside a few times and thought I recognized you."

We had a wonderful time at the competition, but the highlight was the irony of that encounter. I had to travel to Boulder, Colorado to meet a neighbor who lived a quarter of a mile up the road.

Oxon Hill Park in Maryland, right below Washington, D.C. and only minutes from Alexandria, Virginia is the site of a restored working farm acquired and operated by the National Park Service and its Park Rangers. Once, during a walking tour of this historic site, we had paused to admire two beautiful Belgian horses who looked up, saw us and stopped grazing to walk over and visit. As I backed away to get a picture of them with Barbara a passing Ranger greeted us and asked if we were enjoying the tour. We assured her that we were, and complemented her and her fellow Rangers on the wonderful job they were doing here. She thanked us and continued her walk. We proceeded with ours, encountering more Rangers (all female) periodically, with whom we chatted.

When we finished we were at the museum, and when we entered we were greeted by the first Ranger we had met. We talked again, and after listening to her for a bit I asked if she lived in the area, explaining that I was asking because her lovely dialect sounded as if she came from way further south. (In fact, of all the Rangers there her speech was the most "Southern"—and she was the only one who wasn't an African-American.) Turns out I was right: she had moved here recently from Atlanta with her husband, where they'd lived for years, and she hadn't "adapted" yet to the region's speech patterns, a skill she possessed and of which she was quite proud. Then she asked where we lived. "Lower New York State," I said.

"Whay-uh?", she inquired. "Near Port Jervis," I responded.

She persisted. "But whay-uh?" "In Cuddebackville," I told her.

That satisfied her, and she grinned. "Ah lived in Mon'isella"—Monticello, about 20 miles away—"fo' yeahs."

"You're kidding; really?" She nodded. I couldn't believe what I was hearing. There had to be an explanation. "But surely," I said, "you didn't come from there originally."

"Oh, no," she exclaimed. "Ah was boan in the Bronx!"

In-House Tales From The Outhouse

The original summer home was well over 150 years old and did have electricity and plumbing, but a coal-burning Franklin stove in the living room was its only source of heat. This made it necessary to drain the water from the pipes late in autumn, effectively leaving us with no plumbing until spring. We could go occasionally during winter for a day on a weekend to make sure everything was all right with the house but never with the intent to stay overnight. To do so would have obliged us to use the old outhouse, about 100 feet away.

It was a useful facility, though, since one could never guarantee that a well only 18 feet deep would provide a constant supply of water for us and guests throughout a dry summer. As its condition worsened, my father decided to build a new outhouse next spring, and with our help, he did.

It turned out to be much larger and higher than the original and rather attractive, with a shingled roof, pristine wood walls painted white both inside and out and a matching latched door, thankfully missing the carved-out crescent moon that typically announces its purpose. Dad had carefully cut out a small rectangle in the back wall and inserted a pane of etched glass—an elegant touch. The inside only seated two but was wide enough for four, with a floor of small different-colored asphalt tiles obtained as free samples. We were ready for the summer crowd.

One day during dad's vacation a car pulled into the driveway and a black-suited gentleman emerged. Seeing dad and I working on a lawn project he headed towards us, carrying a black book. Not surprisingly, he turned out to be a minister, trying to interest people in converting to his faith. It took a few minutes for my father to respectfully convince him that he was quite content with his beliefs but had a high regard for the minister's, after which the two actually had a very interesting and informative discussion, at the end of which they shook hands.

As the minister was starting to return to his car he paused and looked at my father. "Brother Weismer," he said, mispronouncing our last name in a charming drawl, "I haven't been up north here for too long, so I'm not settled in anywhere yet or even sure whether or not I'll stay in this part of the country. To be honest, I don't have a lot of money, but I do need a place to stay for at least a few weeks. Would you consider letting me rent this bungalow?" He gestured toward the outhouse.

I shot a glance at my father, who somehow managed to keep his composure and not even bat an eyelash as he apologized for having to decline the request, explaining that it was used during the week by friends and family staying over who couldn't be accommodated in the house. The minister understood, and after again wishing us well, entered his car and was soon gone.

Good Dowsers Know What They're Doing

Most "civilized area" residents don't even think about sources of water; they just turn on a faucet and there it is. They know there are underground pipe connections to something somewhere that deliver an apparently inexhaustible flow, barring severe droughts. It's not the same, though, in "the sticks," where families for the most part must depend on water obtained from an underground well on the property. Seems easy enough to do: you hire a well driller who digs until he finds water and turns it into a well. Trouble is, how does he know where to dig? Is there even any water down there and if there is, how far down is it and will the supply be sufficient and constant? I don't know how such questions are answered these days, but half a century ago we were lucky—our well driller was a dowser.

We observed him walk slowly across part of the field, holding a thin fresh-cut "Y"-shaped branch by its two halves above the fork. He gripped them palms-up in his hands, extended sideways slightly to bend out and further separate the halves. At times the upward-facing branch bottom would quiver, even tilt a bit downward, at which point he'd slow down, but if the bottom rose so that it was again facing up or parallel to the ground, he continued. This went on for awhile as we watched, curious about what he was doing. Then, suddenly, he stopped, with the cut end of the branch pointing towards the earth. He backed up and slowly repeated the last few steps; again, the bottom of the branch moved from pointing skyward to straight down. He turned to us and nodded. "This is the spot," he announced. "Your well goes right here!"

Of course, we practically ran across the field to where he was standing, all wanting to try it. He patiently showed each of us how to hold the branch, which he said was from a willow tree and was called a divining rod. Apparently there's some kind of magnet-like force or attraction between the water and the branch that causes a reaction that pulls the cut end towards the water, and the stronger the pull, the more powerful and abundant the source. We each took turns and, incredibly, experienced that force, walking several areas with mixed results but having that "spot" pull on the branch with such power that it could not be broken without backing up to let the force diminish. I was won over; a divining rod works. Can I prove it? Maybe not, but we wound up with a great well that still works.

De Soto Was Discovered In 1946

It was the spring of 1946, less than eight months after the end of World War II. We were on the highway in our sleek new off-white De Soto, happy to be able to enjoy a pleasure trip now that gasoline quotas and rationing for the civilian population were memories. As we headed into lower New York State, the tranquility of the music we were enjoying on the car's radio was shattered by an improvised and unanticipated solo from a police siren behind us. Dad pulled over, puzzled, because his speed had been well within the limit.

The cop got out of his car and approached slowly, studying the car carefully. My father rolled down the window and waited for the officer, who finally approached and politely asked him if he would please step out of the car. He did, and the two engaged in a quiet, amicable conversation for a minute or so, after which they shook hands. The policeman returned to his car and soon drove away.

When dad was back in the car mom asked him what that was all about. Dad gave her a bemused smile. "He apologized for pulling me over because he said I hadn't done anything wrong. He had just wanted to get a good look at the car because he said it was the first new one he'd seen in over four years!"

There is a second story: a few weeks later dad had to be in downtown New York, where parking spots are almost impossible to find, so he entered a parking garage and exited the car. As dad related it, the manager saw the car, came out of his office and directed one of the parking attendants to park the car carefully and not park any car on either side of it for as long as it was there, to be certain that nobody scratched or dented this new car.

Simple Questions Can Be Tough To Answer

We were sitting at the table having lunch one Saturday afternoon when the sun, absent all morning, finally peeked through the clouds, noticeably brightening the room. I got up, walked over to the wall switch and turned the chandelier off.

Son David looked for a few seconds at the ceiling fixture, with its multiple crystal-clear bulbs, then asked, "Daddy, what color is the light when it's off?"

President Eisenhower Got Re-Elected Anyway

Frankly, I was disappointed when Adlai Stevenson lost his bid for the White House in 1952 because I preferred him to Republican rival Dwight Eisenhower, so when the same twosome opposed each other again in 1956 I tried to talk people into voting for Stevenson. However, I wasn't having much success because, let's face it, there really is no such thing as an undecided voter. Then one day a zany idea struck me: by using two legitimate but totally unrelated words comically I might persuade Eisenhower supporters to reconsider their positions. I worked out the idea and, frankly, in at least half the cases in which I used it I felt it actually might have worked. Be assured, though, that first I made sure I knew what each meant.

Earlier that year a classical radio station had aired a guitar piece entitled "Canción de l'Emperador" by a Spaniard "who was lutenist to King Philip II of Spain." I also heard TV and radio journalists refer to Eisenhower as "the incumbent." I now had my weapons, and was ready to use either one. Some targets said nothing, but just looked oddly at me when I made my point. A few who knew the meaning of the words just smiled and said "that's funny." The rest pretended they understood and thanked me for informing them, but there were two unexpected sequences that I'd like to share:

1) One Eisenhower supporter wouldn't even think of altering his support, so I put on an air of mock desperation and blurted out, "But he's a lutenist!" He looked at me and quickly retorted, "I don't give a damn what religion he is, I'm not voting for Stevenson!"

2) Another, a lovely elderly lady, felt Eisenhower had done a lot for the nation and there was no reason not to vote for him again. I looked incredulously at her, shaking my head and said, "But he's an incumbent!" She looked surprised. "Really? I didn't know that." She paused. "Oh, dear; I'll have to think about that. It may not make sense to vote for someone who has trouble getting around."

Out Of The Ashes

It was around 1950 that the St. Joseph's Orphanage was virtually destroyed by fire. Shock waves swept through all of northern New Jersey because not only had it been a well-run, respected institution but an essential one as well. It didn't take long for fundraising and relief efforts to get under way in Teaneck, where we lived, which was only one or two towns away. Being 13 or 14 years old made it easy to relate to these kids, but also it was only four years after the end of World War II, and I'd seen enough pictures of young victims and survivors to want to be part of this crusade. Since we lived just one block away from perhaps the most "prestigious" street in town I decided that I would go door-to-door for donations after school the next day.

It wasn't going as well as I'd hoped. At a few homes nobody responded to the ringing doorbell; at many I was assured that they had already given; at others, though, I was given some coins. I was almost done, which was good because it was now late afternoon and daylight was fading. These were big houses, set well back from the sidewalk, with lots of room between each. Well, just a few more. I reached the next one, pressed the button and listened to the chimes. After a few seconds the door opened and a lady looked at me.

"Yes?", she inquired.

"Hello," I responded cheerfully. "I'm collecting for St. Joseph's Orphanage." Her face clouded and her voice became brusque.

"I'm sorry, but we're not Catholic."

My eyes widened. "Neither am I, ma'am; in fact, I'm Jewish!"

She studied me for a couple of seconds, then turned around and walked away, leaving the front door open. She was gone for about half a minute but when she returned and opened the storm door she was smiling, and extended her other hand.

"Here you are," she said, warmly. "You should be very proud."

I took her offering. "Thank you, ma'am. You're very kind."

I nearly ran back to the curb; I wasn't sure what she'd given me but I knew one thing: it was paper. I looked, and almost fainted.

The lady had given me a five-dollar bill. May not be impressive now, but remember, this was Teaneck, in 1950, and I was just a youngster. And a Jewish one, at that.

Some People Have All The Luck, Thank God

I was almost 36 years old before I took my first trip to Europe; my mother got to go before she was one year old.

Most of her family came to this country from Europe, but some relatives stayed, living in England. Mom's parents could never take an extended vacation because they ran a small but popular grocery store in Brooklyn that couldn't just be closed up for a month; in addition, Mom was the youngest of four children. However, after many years, her mother decided it was time for an overseas trip, and even worked out a way to do it: her husband would run the store and take care of the three older siblings, and she would take the nine-month old baby—my mother—with her. Soon, arrangements were made, tickets purchased, and both sailed to England.

Her family (actually all were her blood relatives) was delighted to see her again after such a long time, catch up on events, meet the newest member and show them around. It was a wonderful visit but, all too soon, after what seemed like barely one exciting blur of a day, it was time for them to return to the United States.

Except that there was a problem: their voyage home had been changed to a later one. They had been bumped.

I knew my mother's diminutive mother as a lovely grandmother, but in her youth it was said she could be feisty at times. Well, being unable to sail on the ship she had selected for the return trip and for which she had specifically purchased tickets apparently had created one of those times. She asked for an explanation, complained and argued, but all to no avail; nothing she said or did changed anything. Every available passenger ticket for the boat she had wanted to take had been sold, and although no reason was given for her having been slighted, there was nothing that could be done; she and her baby would just have to settle for the alternate trip home.

A day or so later they boarded some ship and left England. My grandmother, now calm, had decided that the matter of being treated as a second-class citizen would be pursued from home.

She changed her mind, though, when they docked back in the U.S. and she realized that they had made it, but the ship they were supposed to be on for the return voyage, the *Titanic*, hadn't.

Chapter 13 -

Oddities, Frivolities And Some Points Worth Pondering

Maybe This Will Help To Get Things Done

Life always presents things to be attended to, day and night. Sometimes, more than one issue has to be addressed at the same time, or so it seems. We've all had those days when nothing seems to get done and, worse yet, work just keeps on piling up. Working full-time during the day while going to college at night for years taught me early on how to manage time more effectively, whether on the job, in school or at home. I know it's more easily said than done, but try this; it's worth the few minutes, and it will work:
1) Write down on a piece of paper the tasks that need to be done.
2) Prioritize them—put the most urgent one first.
3) Start doing that first task.

You, Too, Can Be A Chef On Television

It's fun to watch some of the cooking shows on television. The dishes vary and some ingredients are unusual, but for the most part one can't help but feel that almost anyone who's ever seen a kitchen could star in any of those shows and come up with the same results. I say "almost" because three exceptions come to mind: Julia Child, Graham Kerr and Rachael Ray. Each had a show on which courses or meals made were quite different from the other two, but all three had one important and basic thing in common: *they prepared their dishes right in front of you, as you watched.* You even got to see a rare misstep like splashing or spattering or something dropped.

This is in direct contrast to the usual cooking show in which the star, sporting anything from a *toque blanc* to an unfamiliar accent, proceeds to do little more than toss several small containers of pre-measured ingredients into a large bowl and combine them, perhaps adding an already-prepared amount of sauce. The mix is then either put in a pot to be cooked on top of the stove or spread on something raw to be cooked in the oven, both for a given amount of time.

How convenient. How delightful. How ridiculous! How many dishes could any of us prepare if we had a number of unknown, unseen and unmentioned elves backstage to shred that needed eight cups of cabbage for us and mince the four cloves of garlic and trim, peel and cut those five large carrots into small matchsticks and peel, seed and chop four tomatoes and prepare the dressings and sauces and trim the fat or remove the skin or de-vein the shrimp or…

The list is endless. And don't forget the point at which the host decides to add an extra ingredient or two and goes to a kitchen cabinet or pantry to get it. Like Fibber McGee and Molly's closet it's always full and somehow, incredibly, miraculously, always contains what's needed, from a 16-ounce jar of imported pickled Malaysian rhinoceros testicles to a partridge in a pear tree—including the pear tree.

Reality cooking shows are more credible, as The Three Mousse-queteers have shown, and it doesn't matter whether it's fine French cuisine, heart-healthy courses or nicely-balanced 30-minute meals. If you can see even some of each step—slicing, sautéeing, stirring or seasoning to sniffing, savoring or sampling the selected salad, soup, salmon, stew, steak or strawberry shortcake—then you can decide whether or not to attempt the dish yourself and if you do, there should be few if any questions or problems because you saw it all. It was a good learning experience that strengthened your self-confidence. Now you know that you, too, can create a great dish.

Of course, it would be even more helpful if there were a few more elves to do the shopping for all the ingredients you need for this effort, and still be there afterwards to scrub all the dirty pots, pans, dishes and utensils you created along with your masterpiece.

Handling Distraction Also Takes Skill

The golf pro is on the 16th green, ready to attempt a relatively straightforward 15-foot putt for birdie in this final round of a major tournament. Two competitors awaiting their turn watch from yards away, silent and motionless. There are no spectators. You can hear a pin drop. He lines up the shot and is just about ready to start his putt when a roar is heard from the crowd gathered far away at the 18th hole, cheering something there. He stiffens and steps back, his face showing undisguised annoyance at a distraction that shattered his concentration. Soon, having managed to regain his composure, he realigns the shot and is able to continue his attempt to make it.

Meanwhile, somewhere else, a well-played tennis match is in the fifth set. The stadium crowd, politely silent during each volley, has begun rooting for the underdog, who was not expected to play this well and actually stand a chance of beating his number two-seeded rival to move on to the quarter-finals. The rising excitement takes the form of cheers and shouts of encouragement for the Spaniard to hang in there as he awaits his opponent's serve. The Russian leans forward with ball in hand, ready to begin but instead straightens up, mumbles something, and backs up a few steps, waiting, his intense level of concentration destroyed. A second later a voice over the loudspeakers firmly demands "Quiet, please," followed by "Thank you" when the crowd obliges. His self-control restored, the serve can be made for the match to proceed.

I don't get it. It's *his* serve; he's in command and controls the play. If crowd noise keeps him from serving, how is it that neither player is bothered in the slightest by the grunts and groans they emit while the volley is in progress? At first I thought one of them was constipated and the other had hemmorhoids. And lady players are even worse. Watch them on TV. When the moaning and shrieking start just close your eyes, listen and try not to imagine a lovemaking scene reaching climax.

Golf is no better. After all, whether driving or putting, it's one person with a club combating a small, unarmed defenseless ball. If some noise a quarter of a mile away is enough to make that person distraught just imagine what baseball would do to him. Picture this: It's the top of the eighth, with two runners on base, two out and the team at bat trailing by just one run. It's a crucial game late in the season; the opposing team is not only winning but ahead in the standings, in second place by a game. And now it's his turn to bat.

He steps up to the plate, sets himself in the batter's box, looks towards the pitcher and takes a few practice swings. The pitcher, being on an elevated mound, seems high and awfully close. The batter sees him but it's late afternoon; the playing field between first and third is in shade in such a manner that the mound is in sunlight but the batter's box isn't. Suddenly an organ is heard over the loudspeakers playing "The Mexican Hat Dance," to which 56,000 screaming fans applaud in rhythm. Most are wearing white blouses or T-shirts, especially in the outfield stands beyond the pitcher's mound where the hitter must look, concentrate and try to isolate from dozens of waving white flags a small approaching missile leaving the sunlight, entering the shadow zone and curving towards his head at 97 miles an hour. Oh, yes—he also must decide whether to swing and how, so as to not only make contact but with enough accuracy to produce a base hit. So many decisions and distractions, so little time. What to do? Realizing the overwhelming challenges he's facing, he takes the only course of action he can.

He backs out of the batter's box, scowls and asks the umpire to request the organist to stop playing "The Mexican Hat Dance."

Why Hurt The Environment *And* Waste Money?

A car parks outside an establishment—it could be a post office, a convenience store, an ATM or whatever. He gets out and goes inside, leaving the motor running. A few minutes later he emerges, having accomplished whatever he intended to do, and drives off.

A shopper enters a mall and drives towards the place she wishes to patronize. Cruising the parking lot, she heads for the row that's closest. Reaching it, she turns into it and proceeds slowly, looking ahead. She's already passed several open spaces but they're still relatively distant, and she'd have to walk about 100 feet, maybe a bit more, to get to her destination. Suddenly she sees a shopper just ahead, walking towards her and pushing a full cart. She puts the car in neutral and waits, leaving the motor running, figuring that the woman pushing the cart is headed for a car that's already parked and a lot closer to the stores. Sure enough, the walking shopper reaches the parked car, fumbles for keys, opens the trunk, and begins to unload the cart. It takes a few minutes, but eventually it's emptied and pushed out of the way. The shopper then enters the car and sits for what seems like another couple of minutes fumbling around inside her purse, checking her hair and makeup in the rear-view mirror, belting herself in, then finally starting the car, carefully backing out and driving off. Triumphantly, the waiting woman drives her car past four other parked cars on each side of her to the open space and pulls in. By being patient for just those few minutes she saved herself at least 40 feet of extra walking.

We've all seen these things, and more than once. Don't these people realize how much needless pollution they're contributing to the atmosphere nationwide each day and how many gas dollars are being wasted while this environmental damage continues?

A Spoiled Opportunity, Litter-Ally

It's such a breathtaking scene: majestic snow-capped mountains overlooking sylvan fields of wild grasses and flowers that surround a crystal-clear lake, shimmering right in front of you.

In the middle of which is a large white styrofoam coffee cup, lying on its side.

You sigh, turn off the camera and head back to your car. So much for that perfect camera shot.

Moral: *Please* don't litter.

It Still Adds Up To The Needed Number Of Years

Many companies provide employee pensions, a benefit that grew under unions decades ago when a young adult out of school would get a job with a firm and typically remain until retirement at age 65. There were conditions: usually, one had to last at least 25 years, but having done so one could augment Social Security income with that of a pension which, from some firms, could be generous—perhaps rewarding years of faithful service for relatively low pay (Prentice-Hall and Sears, Roebuck are two examples that come to mind).

Most firms kept their part of the bargain. There were a few well-publicized ones that fired workers nearing the 25-year mark but this was by far the exception. The system worked until the last half of the 20th century when technology, the pace and style of life and its demands soared, destroying traditional loyalties between companies and their employees. New companies were emerging everywhere, offering once non-existent opportunities to well-qualified or well-educated specialists who could now work and live anywhere. It was not unusual now for a worker to stay less than 10 years on a job before leaving for a more promising or rewarding opportunity. A good pension plan was no longer an attractive job benefit—after all, how many engineers going to work for a high-tech firm were going to stick around for 40 years? Maybe it was time to change.

It didn't take long for many companies to reduce the number of years for pension eligibility from 25 to 10 and, a few years later, to as low as five—a huge improvement, but still not totally acceptable. I understand the need for such a system and I favor it, but why not simply make it one year? Many development or project-oriented specialists are forced to find new employment after a three- or four-year contract ends or expires. These people may work for 40 years, like teachers or other union-protected workers, but why should they be denied pension benefits because those 40 years included 10 or 12 jobs instead of only one or two? It's stealing, and is as dishonest as a company prematurely firing current employees, or reducing or canceling their pension benefits to save a few bucks.

"Get A Free Turkey" Is Not Always Fair Game

Many supermarkets offer shoppers a free Thanksgiving turkey for shopping with them and spending just $300 (it used to be $250) over a specified nine-week period between late September and late November, using the same customer card. This is fine—if you're shopping for a family of four or five and perhaps have a pet or two. I've seen such shoppers spend over $120 in just one shopping visit. Many wind up with two, even three free turkeys (which is allowed) and donate the extras to charities and churches that provide dinners for the poor, a very thoughtful, admirable and beneficial practice.

But what about older shoppers whose children no longer live at home, leaving just the two of them or, worse yet, just one person who is widowed, divorced or otherwise single? Such people rarely even approach $300, much less reach it, so unless they cheat and give their cards to heavy-shopping friends who already have a free turkey and ask them to use it instead of their own when shopping, these elders never accumulate enough points to get a free turkey.

This is totally unfair. Why can't such shoppers be given at least a proportionate percentage of credit towards the sale price of a turkey based on the dollar amount they've accumulated during the nine-week period? In other words, if that shopper has accumulated, say, $150 towards the required $300 by the end of the nine-week period and wants to buy a turkey, let her, but reduce the sale price by 50%. That's both fair and considerate, and doesn't exactly hurt customer loyalty and attitude towards the place.

Sometimes It Pays To Be Second-Best

It was unquestionably the most beautiful tree imaginable and had been for as long as anyone could remember. One older gentleman recalled being there when the tree was planted and how quickly it got to be taller than he was, yet so lush and perfectly formed that he and his pals used it as "home" when they played "hide and seek" some 60 years ago. Now it had become an 85-foot-tall Norway spruce, a model of perfection unrivalled by anything in the area. It had survived severe dry spells, rains, floods, winds and the terrible ravages of the 1938 hurricane. And it had withstood these forces of nature for 70 years.

Seventy years of strength, survival and beauty brought to an end in minutes as a team of workers with chainsaws cuts it down, loads it on a flatbed truck and transports it to New York City to be set up in Rockefeller Center with colored lights in time for the Christmas season, where millions can view its twinkling sparkle for six weeks without wondering what happens to it after New Year's Eve or noticing that right now it's slowly dying of suffocation and hunger.

Leave The Continental To Fred Astaire

Most good American motels (such as those in the Choice chain) offer a complimentary Continental breakfast with your stay. These can range from as little as a juice, breads and rolls, donuts, coffee and tea to more typical ones that offer several varieties of juices, teas, milks and creams (some flavored), hot and dry cereals, waffles, bagels, pancakes, English muffins, many choices of toppings, brownies, cupcakes, buns, cinnamon twirls, yogurts and fresh fruits. A few even have a cook preparing flapjacks and eggs sunny-side-up or scrambled, with sausage or bacon.

Now I'll admit, I haven't been to Europe in many years, but I do remember that wherever we stayed—from hotels and *pensiones* to remodeled nun's quarters—the morning began with a sophisticated Continental breakfast, typically consisting of a demitasse-sized cup of hot syrupy Turkish-style coffee topped with boiling-hot milk that you stirred with a trowel to combine, accompanied by a roll which had also been touring Europe for a few days.

I guess what I don't understand is why any American hotelier would want to refer to his bounteous breakfast by a European name that evokes thoughts of a Barmecide feast.

Personalized Plastic Containers

They were in a booth at a Perkins restaurant, waiting for the breakfast specials they had ordered to arrive. A couple of moments later the waitress delivered them, still steaming, and set them down: scrambled eggs, bacon and toast for the young man, eggs sunny side up and toast for his pretty companion, and a pot of coffee. The man rubbed his hands together, smiled, and proceeded to pour coffee into each of their mugs. From a bowl of small creamer containers he took a couple for himself, opened them and added them to his cup; the lady did the same for her coffee. Reaching across to the far side of the table she selected a small container of orange marmalade, peeled off the top cover and applied some with a knife to one of the four triangular toast wedges on her plate. He did the same to a piece of his toast except that he preferred Concord grape jelly. They then enjoyed some coffee before getting started on their respective egg dishes. Being both coffee lovers as well as hungry, it wasn't long before their astute waitress came by with a second pot of fresh-brewed coffee. Half an hour later breakfast was over; they had really enjoyed it, especially the much-needed wakeup coffee. Now they were ready to pay and leave.

Each had consumed four half-slices of toast with most of a container of jelly for each, along with three mugs of coffee with two creamers per mug. That's three jelly containers and six creamers each, or nine single-use plastic containers per person. The place has over 50 tables, all in use except two or three being readied to accommodate those waiting by the front doors to be seated. Each table has at least two people; many hosted a family of four. It's probably fair to put the number of breakfasters at 150, an average of three per table.

Let's assume that the couple referred to was excessive in their consumption of coffee and jellied toast. At the other extreme there are those who prefer coffee black or don't drink any, or who wanted pancakes for breakfast instead of eggs and toast. To be fair, we'll use an average: instead of 150 diners using 9 containers each, let's cut it in half and make it 75 diners x 9 containers (or 150 diners x 4.5). Either way, the total number of containers used comes to 675.

And that's just by one wave of people on a typical non-vacation-season Tuesday morning at 9:00 o'clock. How many hungry people preceded them? How many more will come in to eat over the next couple of hours? How many more restaurants and diners are there in the area? In the county? In the state? In the nation?

And that's only two container types. What about shampoo and conditioner bottles found in motels and hotels, and other kinds too numerous to mention? All told, there must be millions of these variegated one-time containers used each day throughout the world. And let's not forget their peel-off or screw-off tops.

Oh, by the way, did I forget to mention that *not one of these types of plastic containers or their tops is recyclable?*

Can I Get A Cell-Phone Plan For Cable TV?

Maybe I don't like all the TV channels that satellite or cable TV providers offer. I don't want premium channels; basic cable is fine. I can skip all the women's channels, especially the weepy, male-bashing and home-shopping ones. I don't watch 10 hours of sports every weekend day any more than I watch hours of speeches from House of Representatives or Senate members. I don't need foreign-language or religious stations. However, I do enjoy several basic channels, even though they're disgustingly saturated with ads and, worse yet, promos for forthcoming shows, some of which are weeks away. So here's a thought: how about offering a choice of plans for viewers based on monthly viewing hours instead of a flat plan rate?

If I want to watch, say, up to 100 hours a month of basic channels, offer me such a plan. If I watch only 72 hours, that's my problem—I signed up for an up-to-100-hour plan, so I pay in full for that month and if I exceed the maximum, I pay a reasonable surcharge for the extra hours. Other plans can offer greater or fewer hours, but at least there's a choice. To make it even more attractive, give a 10% credit for unused hours, so that if I watch only 72 out of the 100 hours I signed up for I get credit for 10 of them or they're carried over to next month, which now gives me 110 for that month.

If that's unacceptable, then offer me a plan based on a number of basic channels of my choice—say, 40; if I don't want that many, offer me 20. If I want those 20 to include such networks as, say, ABC, CBS, NBC, Discovery, local Public Television, History, Turner Classic Movies, Travel, Comedy Central, TV Land, Food, Hallmark, Spike, Fox, Weather, CNN, ESPN, TNT and two others, give them to me and charge me a flat monthly fee for just those 20.

Or wouldn't that be profitable enough for you service providers?

Why Is This Cop Allowed To Get Away With It?

This is a direct quote from an article that appeared in the Friday, October 19, 2007 "Times Herald-Record" (Middletown, NY); only the perpetrator's last name has been omitted here:

"**Goshen** – A former Tuxedo Park cop pleaded guilty yesterday to official misconduct, a misdemeanor, for falsifying timecards that netted him more than $40,000 in unearned pay."

"John R_____ will not have to pay restitution under the plea agreement but could spend two months in county jail and get five years' probation when he's sentenced Dec. 17."

That's over $20,000 a month—the equivalent of $250,000 a year! I know a lot of hard-working people who'd be quite willing to have a roof over their heads and three meals a day provided and paid for by the state in return for getting away with a crime and not having to repay ripped-off taxpayers (and this guy's a cop!). Hell, for that kind of money, *I'd* even consider serving 2 months in a nice, clean local jail, with possible time off for good behavior.

Medical Coverage Is Both Anatomically And Geographically Incorrect

Recently I completed treatment involving major dental surgery in stages for a problem that, if ignored, would have caused the loss of most of my teeth. Fortunately, all were saved, but the cost to me exceeded $12,000 and wasn't covered under any medical plan. It seems that "teeth" are not part of the human body—that's "dental," not "medical."

Eye examinations are usually covered, but if you need corrective lenses of any kind—those that improve astigmatism or near-sightedness, or ones with precisely-placed prisms to correct serious double-vision problems—they're not covered either, and they can cost hundreds of dollars, excluding frames. Seems that "eyes," too, are unrelated to human anatomy—that's "visual," not "medical."

At this rate, how long before treating kids will also be excluded from coverage because, after all, that's "child care," not "medical." Yet the use of Viagra, even for known sex offenders, was covered long before mammograms and birth-control pills for women were. Breast implants, no; that's cosmetic surgery. But Viagra is worthy of medical coverage? Where and when does this nonsense stop?

There's something wrong with a system that allows almost half of our nation to be uninsured or unable to pay for medical care, yet donates millions of dollars worth of services to immigrants (legal or otherwise) for problems ranging from delicate eye or brain surgery to separating co-joined twins. And heaven forbid that the superior coverage in several other countries be brought up; such people are immediately accused (and you know by whom) of being socialists.

The system must be improved, but when? How? By whom?

The First Things I Must Do When I'm President

Women continue to object to being treated as mere sex objects in a male-dominated society, a topic that must be addressed nationally. That's why when I'm elected our country's new leader my first task must be to get Congress to change all laws that require females to solicit sex or other favors, pose in various stages of nudity for magazine covers and centerfolds, work at Hooter's or be porn stars. Next we must overturn all statutes that leave women no choice but to be humiliated by having to wear skimpy clothing starting at age 12 that forces them to display cleavage and reveal generous sections of other above-groin areas. Finally, I shall demand the repeal of any legal proclamations stating that women's lib ends at the wallet, thereby giving women the freedom to pick up the tab for the evening when out on a date with a man.

The Clever Conniving Convenience Of Contrived Corporate Chronometers

When a new trend sweeps the nation, companies can produce products to meet these needs almost overnight. Remember when people clamored for whole- or multi-grain foods? Manufacturers of cereals, pasta, breads and such created entire lines of reformulated products, complete with new packaging, and had them in stores for purchase in as little as six weeks, accompanied by a blitz of TV and magazine ads. And apparently it's just as easy to do the same for anything from complex electronic gadgetry to cosmetics. But ask these companies to reduce emissions from a chimney or to stop dumping waste into a river and somehow such challenges take from seven to 12 years to accomplish.

Insurance companies are very efficient at collecting money owed them (premiums) by the due date specified, but if as a client you submit a claim you're almost guaranteed at least a three-week wait. Why? Simple—it's money in their pockets. Your $1,000 claim may not seem like much, but multiply that by 100,000 additional claims for the same amount and the payout amounts to one hundred *million* dollars! If that money can remain in its investment portfolio for just a few more weeks, the company's assets will have increased by about another $500,000!

Banks are just as slimy. Even in this computer age, deposit a check—even if it's one from another bank, or from someone within your state—and you'll be told it takes 5 to 10 *business* days for it to clear (weekends don't count). But let your account drop below its required minimum monthly balance even for a few hours and you'll be assessed a $10 or $15 penalty for the month. Worse yet, should that "someone within your state" whose check you deposited have insufficient funds and the check bounces, *both of you* are penalized.

It was an unusually frigid night in California. By morning your supermarket has raised the price of lettuces and posted a sign apologizing for having to do so because of the unexpected cold weather conditions. The same happens to citrus fruits when Florida encounters such weather. The problem is that these products were already on the shelves, so why not wait until the next shipment arrives and then raise prices?

The price of a barrel of oil rises because of seasonal or increased demands, rumors or just plain outright corporate greed. Again, with previously delivered gasoline already sitting in the tanks, the price per gallon at the pump will increase within a day or two. So why is a drop in oil prices not reflected in the price at the pump for at least a week?

Not everything is negative, though, so to be fair, let's applaud a couple of positive examples.

Utility rates increase steadily by many dollars a month, but let an investigation determine that as customers we were overcharged for a few months or some such period of time and the company will act quickly to reduce our next month's bill, often by as much as $2!

A real estate or school tax increase of 7%, costing a household hundreds of dollars annually, is considered "a slight increase," but a reduction amounting to a refund of $21 per family is recognized as "a whopping tax cut."

Everybody Uses The "D" Word

There are many negative nouns and adjectives used to describe both erratic behavioral qualities and the people who exhibit them. What's interesting, though, is how many of these descriptive words begin with the letter "d." Consider the following:

Dingbat, dork(y), ditz(y), dweeb, dumbbell, dimwit, dumbass, dickhead, drip, dysfunctional, disturbed, disoriented, disillusioned, demented, deranged, destabilized, disconnected.

And I'll bet you can probably think of even more.

What Does A Chicken Use To Cross The Road?

This is another true story that you just can't make up, but I put it here rather than in the prior chapter to illustrate why so many "d" words are needed. You choose the ones that apply.

A group of us at a party were seated at the dinner table when our hostess arrived with a platter of nicely-prepared chicken breasts and legs. When one of the ladies was asked which she preferred, she informed everyone that she eats chicken breasts but not chicken legs because "I don't know where they've walked. I also don't eat bologna because it's made with chicken lips." When my wife Barbara pointed out that chickens don't have lips, the woman (who happened to be a teacher) assured her that they do and steadfastly refused to even consider the possibility that she might be incorrect.

The "Stealth" Bomber

The "Stealth" bomber was a relatively large aircraft capable of flying about 600 miles per hour, whose unique design and use of components made it hard to identify on radar because the blip it created more resembled that of a bird in flight than an airplane.

The man watching the radar screen at a military base in a foreign country sees an unusual blip suddenly appear on his monitor. After observing it for a few seconds he determines that even though it's flying at 600 miles an hour its size identifies it as a bird. Therefore he doesn't report it because, obviously, it has to be either a pigeon carrying a letter or a stork delivering a newborn baby.

How To Save Money And Still Be The First To Enjoy A Live Concert

You're sitting in a balcony section at Carnegie Hall, enjoying a live performance. A good friend of yours in Brisbane, Australia is able to share the pleasure of this concert with you, thanks to the fact that it's being broadcast simultaneously worldwide.

Since electricity travels near light speed (186,300 miles per second) and sound travels through air at only 1,088 *feet* per second, guess which of the two of you actually gets to hear the music first.

There Is No Downside To A Good Comeuppance

Well-known businessman John F. Cuneo lived in a grand family estate near Libertyville, Illinois, about an hour north of Chicago. Now the Cuneo Museum and Gardens, we had an opportunity while visiting friends to go there, see the grounds and be given a guided indoor tour. Unfortunately we had a tour guide reminiscent of an old-fashioned schoolmarm, whose recitative style of presentation suggested that not only was she bored but also resentful of having to take yet another group of troglodytes through a mansion whose opulence only she could fully appreciate.

Questions from the group were not encouraged, and although the few that were asked were rather astute the condescending tone used to answer them soon stopped all. We were happy to simply absorb the magnificence of the architecture and contents, all of which came from centuries-old European mansions and churches. As the guide identified some outstanding pieces, she repeatedly informed us that Mr. Cuneo was able to purchase them and have them shipped here, since he was a wealthy man. The group's growing annoyance with her was soon voiced in an increasing number of murmured negative comments and amusing asides as the tour progressed.

When we finally returned to the point from which we had started our guide informed us that this was the end of the tour, suggested that we see the gardens, reminded us not to touch anything, then asked if anyone had any questions. I raised my hand.

"Yes," she acknowledged, nodding towards me. "You have a question."

"Thank you; yes," I responded. "I believe you indicated that Mr. Cuneo was a wealthy man."

"Yes, that's correct; he was."

I continued. "Well, then I don't understand. If he was so rich, how come the house is filled with nothing but used furniture?"

Got her. She was caught off-guard and couldn't come up with a response, but better yet, our group loved it. A few even applauded as they laughed. Got her—and she deserved it.

The Monitor And The Merry Mack

I can't help but laugh when I watch television shows like "*CSI: New York*". Oh, sure, the technology does exist for them to solve a crime based on a fleck of dandruff, but first you have to find that fleck of dandruff. Only on TV can one of these wizards spot it by a streetlight half a block away, retrieve it, look at it and know that it came from a man in his late 20s who lost it while it was raining because it's wet, then look up and calculate that, based on where in the street it was found, he had to have been on the 17th floor, third window in from the right, and must have lost it when he leaned out the window to see if it was raining and scratched his head, which makes him the probable perpetrator of the crime being investigated.

"*World's Wildest Police Videos,*" I think, is a far more realistic example of police intelligence. Every situation featured is typically the same: a speeding or erratic driver either ignores the police or, having been pulled over, simply drives off while being tested or questioned by them. Of course, this menace must be taken off the road because innocent people could be put at risk, so the police turn their car's siren on and the chase begins. Soon, anywhere from one to six police cars are pursuing a driver who somehow is always able to outmaneuver and out-race them for miles on major highways and local streets *while under the influence of alcohol*. Sometimes a news or police helicopter is included, taping the action from the air. Eventually the chase does end, the driver being apprehended after blowing a tire or trying to take a shortcut through the woods. But how many dozens of other drivers and passengers did the cops put at an even greater risk of death or serious injury on that highway? How about when the pursuit is in a populated area and causes the fleeing driver to approach an intersection, ignore a stop sign or red light and drive straight through, sometimes after sideswiping a few parked cars? Why couldn't the cops broadcast the car's description, license, location and direction to other cops and ask them to set up something *up ahead* instead of just adding to the number of vehicles in pursuit and creating such risky danger? Whatever happened to the old "Calling all cars—be on the lookout for..." that we all remember from old-time movies? At times I feel like I'm watching *"The Keystone Cops,"* except this is reality.

Then again, perhaps a new TV show that combines all of these features, entitled *"America's Funniest Science Fiction Police Videos,"* would garnish unprecedented ratings.

Smile Though Your Piles Are Bleeding

You wanna have fun? Some day, dress up in a dark business suit so that you look like an executive and walk into a Madison Avenue ad agency with an unwavering shit-eating grin on your face. When someone asks if they can help you, ask to see the executive in charge of new client accounts and, while you're waiting, converse pleasantly with the receptionist and anyone else there, occasionally throwing back your head and laughing for no apparent reason but never losing that broad basic smile. Sooner or later you will attract attention and arouse feelings ranging from curiosity and amusement to uneasiness and fear, and someone—perhaps the executive—will ask you why you're constantly smiling, since it looks strange. After assuming a hurt look, state that you're puzzled by that comment and explain why, pointing out that that's all you see in ads these days, even those promoting such things as home nursing for Alzheimer's patients or herpes-preventing products featuring already-infected females. Tell him you assumed it was an effective way to impress people and win them over, so if it worked for ad agencies it should work for you, too, or else why would all ads use such an otherwise senseless and irritating approach?

He may have you thrown out, but hey, at worst, you may have given him something to think about; at best, you may have inspired a Renaissance resulting in a completely new concept, causing you to be remembered in time as the Father of Bearable Advertisements.

Sometimes The Lord Knows More Than We Do

Many believe that each of us has a soul. I can live with that—in fact, I can even die with that. Maybe that's why, when the good Lord informed us that we were created from dust He added that unto dust shall we return. Perhaps it takes time for an entrapped soul to escape and be free to exist spiritually for eternity. Burial just might be the key to immortality, and I'll be damned (figuratively and literally) if I'm going to lose it all by being cremated.

All People Know Who And What They Are

For many years my wife and I were volunteer educators (a term I prefer to "docent"), giving local-history tours to hundreds of groups of school kids as well as to various "special" groups of youngsters and adults. From those experiences as well as friendships and other interaction with people worldwide we've learned a lot about how people think of themselves and prefer to be seen:

1) Blacks do *not* like being described as "African-Americans"—especially those who come from or were born in the Caribbean.
2) Do *not* ask an Oriental, "You're what—Chinese or Japanese?" There are other possibilities, such as Vietnamese, Korean, etc.
3) Many darker-skinned people speaking English with a familiar accent are from India, true, but many are Pakistanis; don't assume.
4) Whites don't like being referred to as "honkies" or "gringos."
5) "Native Americans" hate that term; if necessary, refer to them as "indigenous people" but, if possible, refer to them by their tribal name—for example, "he's a member of the Lakota tribe." (By the way, only if he's 100 per cent "pure" can he be called "a Lakotan.")
6) Depending on the degree of severity, people in wheelchairs are either handicapped or crippled, but either way they hate being regarded as being "physically challenged." As one youngster put it, "I'm handicapped; nobody's 'challenging' me to stand up and run."
7) Similarly, many adults and kids in two "special" groups were quite specific about how they wished to be referred to. While they appreciated my thoughtful and well-meant intentions they made it perfectly clear that "we're retarded, not mentally challenged."

Above all, however, is this most common, unifying perception: *everyone* born or living in the U.S. considers himself or herself *an American* and despises divisive "politically correct" terminology. And actually this attitude makes sense, if you think about it. After all, if a man has been a resident of Brussels since his grandparents moved there from Sydney and became citizens, does anyone refer to him as "an Australian-Belgian"? Or, if you want to go one step further, if you believe in the science of anthropology and/or the Old Testament, wouldn't that make us all African-Americans?

How To Communicate With The French

One of the many advantages of traveling abroad on a group tour is that you don't have to be concerned with that country's language, a major consideration. If you travel on your own you'd better be fluent, because even if you know a few expressions or words there's still the risk of an incorrectly pronounced or chosen word, resulting in anything from confusion to an unintended insult. Besides, even if you successfully complete your inquiry you now face the task of having to listen to and simultaneously translate a response which, it seems, is usually spoken at 800 to 900 words per minute.

Historically, the French have been the people most resented and disliked by Americans because, among other reasons, they refuse to speak English, even though we all know dammed well they can (if you don't think so, try leaving a restaurant after having enjoyed a great meal without paying your bill). But unless you're visiting a country with an extremely difficult or complex language (such as Finland or China) there is a solution: just politely inform the person you wish to talk to that you don't speak his language and ask if by chance he speaks English. Believe me, it works. Barbara and I first tried it in Montreal several times and were amazed at how quickly cloudy faces were replaced by ones of sunshine and warmth. When friends tell us they're going to France and are concerned about their inability to speak French we share our Montreal experiences with them and actually tell them what we said and suggest they try it:

"Pardon, monsieur (madame); je ne parle pas français tres bien.
Par chance, parlez-vous anglais?"
(I'm sorry, sir (madam); I don't speak French very well.
By chance, do you speak English?)

Without exception, everyone responded positively in English, pleased that we at least attempted to communicate in their language. I then thanked them and told them how glad I was that they spoke English because, as my French teacher told me in high school,

"Vous parlez français comme une vache espagnol!"
(You speak French like a Spanish cow!)

It worked; they laughed; the cold war was over. It's also worked for our Paris-bound friends, and I'll bet it will work for you, too.

Is Everybody Drinking The Water?

When we lived in New Jersey, sections of the state were having problems with the purity of drinking water, so whenever we would hear or read about something illogical, hard to believe or just plain stupid we'd look at each other in disbelief and ask, "Is everybody drinking the water?" There are various kinds of "somethings," but one type that seems to crop up periodically involves mail-in rebates. These can be quite beneficial to consumers when there's a decent amount of money involved, making such participation worthwhile, but some, quite frankly, are simply puzzling. The following is just one example out of several lately:

A K-Mart sales circular for the week of March 23rd through 29th, 2008 featured two Hyponex products. The first was a 40-lb. bag of topsoil, on sale for $1.29 *after a 60 cent mail-in rebate*; the other was a 40-lb. bag of organic humus and manure, on sale for $1.69 *after a 60-cent mail-in rebate.*

Unless someone's buying a few bags, why would anyone spend 41 cents in postage to get back 60 cents, a net of just 19 cents? And why would Hyponex spend yet another 41 cents to mail the rebate? That's 82 cents to refund 60 cents to a customer. Is that worth it? Why not just sell the products for $1.29 and $1.69, respectively?

Don't Fall For The Old "Party" Line

There is always that one employee—someone you work with, or for—whose demeanor is consistently brusque and whose comments about the job, fellow workers or the company are always critical, negative, and delivered in a sneering or nasty tone of voice without regard for anyone within earshot. But what I never understood is, if someone points out the fact that this griper is always that way and never has anything good to say about anything, someone else will be there to defend such behavior with something like, "Oh, he's not that way at all outside of work. You ought to see him at a party; he's totally different. *That's* the *real* John."

Don't believe it. If someone's a prick with ears for eight hours and a social charmer the rest of the day you can't know who "the real John" is. Never trust such people, much less befriend them.

Why Aren't All Great Americans Honored?

George Washington, our first President (and certainly one of the greatest), used to be singularly honored by the observance of his birthday on February 22ⁿᵈ—a day that was once referred to jokingly as "Birthington's Washday." Similarly, February 12ᵗʰ became still another reason to go out shopping instead of to school or work, this time to commemorate the birth of The Great Emancipator, President Abraham Lincoln. Although we've been blessed with many more outstanding leaders who were in the right place at the right time (Theodore Roosevelt, Franklin D. Roosevelt and Harry Truman are just a few that come to mind), their birthdays have never been established as days of official national celebration. On the contrary, just the opposite has occurred: we've lost the individuality of our honorees to an eponymous collective known as President's Day.

Which is fine. After all, if the day each President entered this world became a *cause célèbre* we'd now have over 40 days off. Worse, the reason for the establishment of the holiday—to salute *achievements*, not birth—would be lost: Warren G. Harding would be considered as worthy of recognition as Dwight D. Eisenhower. Having just one day to acknowledge *all* Presidents is good because each of us can select those we consider worthy of our respect and remember them with gratitude in a personally meaningful way.

And this is why I'm not happy with Martin Luther King, Jr. Day.

Indisputably, Dr. King's efforts to improve the perception and treatment of minorities helped better us as a nation and put us on a path of understanding still being traveled. The appreciation of the man and his work continues to grow, as well it should, but this icon is only one out of hundreds to whom we are indebted—some nearly forgotten. Who remembers Dr. Ephraim MacDowell, the first man ever to attempt a surgical operation (he succeeded against all odds)? How dark would life be without Thomas Edison? How many of us would be in a wheelchair if Dr. Jonas Salk had not developed the polio vaccine? Would we even be a nation without our Founding Fathers? The number of categories and honorees is staggering; that's why we need a special day in the spirit of President's Day to acknowledge them all as a nation and many of them as individuals.

We need a Great Americans Day, and we need it soon.

How About Just A Few More Hors D'oeuvres?

1) What do you say to someone who is willing to give his life to live to be 100 years old?
2) When a joke begins with something like: "This guy is told by his doctor that he only has six months to live," never tell it to anyone over the age of 70.
3) All good marriages involve sacrifices and concessions. In my case, I had to give up being divorced.

4) I agree that government shouldn't get involved in religious matters, but who else in a city can suspend alternate-side-of-the-street parking on Good Friday or Yom Kippur?

5) Being one of millions of youngsters growing up in a large city, having to endure hot summers surrounded by heat-reflecting structures and streets, how in hell were we able to survive without bottled water?

6) On the other hand, the reason that none of us youngsters grew up walking like Quasimodo is that backpacks were for soldiers, not school kids.

7) NAFTA (the North American Free Trade Agreement): as consumers and shoppers, we love it, but as American workers and citizens, how can we possibly support it?

8) When you listen to the weather report and the temperature is given, remember: that's always what it is *in shade*. On a sunny day it's actually a few degrees warmer outside.

9) My father saw through the pretentious ostentation of wannabees in some "prestigious" new neighborhoods—or as he described them, people "with a Cadillac in the driveway and an empty refrigerator inside."

10) Some recipes call for an ingredient that not everyone might like, but one TV show featured a dish that called for a prepared ingredient that I wouldn't touch with a ten-foot pole (or an eight-foot hungarian): blue-cheese ice cream.

11) If you want to enjoy food more, eat only one selection at a time. If you're eating a steak with a baked potato and green beans, don't take a piece of meat and follow it with a forkful of beans and then a forkful of potato. Eat all of each separately, and the tastiness of each will last longer.

12) From our travels, the best state drivers are from Oregon and Washington; the worst are from Massachusetts.

13) I have little admiration for today's unions but without them we'd be back in the days of virtual enslavement of the poor by upper-class robber barons in the blink of an eye.

14) Senior citizens seem to comprise the most gullible group of victims preyed upon by con artists and scam masters. Is common sense the first thing one loses in old age or did it take them all those years to become so perfectly stupid?

15) Always have pencil and paper handy so if an idea suddenly hits you (whether for a solution to a problem or a subject worthy of a book) you won't have to berate yourself when you get back home or wake

up the next morning and can't remember what that inspirational thought was.

16) It's late in a crucial baseball game. The batter approaches home plate and crosses himself; the pitcher bows his head and points heavenward. Which one does God favor?

17) People describe a vehicle problem as "this loud noise from the right rear side" or "the left headlight's out," but what's "right" or "left?" Are you driving or seeing the car from the outside? Why not just identify the problem as "from the rear of the passenger's side" or "on the driver's side?"

18) A woman was asked yesterday what making love with her husband has been like, and her whining response was that it's been hard lately. Excuse me, but isn't that the way it should be every time you make love?

19) Cans of soup broth used to be 15½ ounces, yielding 2 cups; now many are down to 14 ounces, yet the number of cups is still shown as "about 2." So how is it that four 14-ounce cans provide only 6½ cups instead of "about 8"?

20) A TV show you're watching is unexpectedly interrupted to report a breaking news story or crisis. Aren't we lucky that such events never occur during a commercial break?

21) A devastating Kansas tornado destroyed most homes in an area but left a few others untouched. No one died, and the victims thanked God for watching over them and sparing them. Sorry, but if the Lord so loved you, why did the tornado occur in the first place?

22) Supposedly, no one dreams in color. Says who? I know I have, many times; how about you?

23) When one thinks of a nation that's neutral during wartime, Switzerland invariably comes to mind, but if that's true, how is it that world-renowned Jewish tenor Josef Schmidt died during World War II *in a Swiss concentration camp?*

24) Of course women are more gifted than men; that's because we keep buying them presents.

25) I'll never understand why so many European and Russian Jews, having endured persecution for centuries, emigrated to the United States and converted to Christianity.

26) Here's a philosophical (gross!) question: If you're standing up to your chin in urine, brine and feces, and someone throws a bucket of vomit at you, would you duck?

27) When gangster Al Capone died he reputedly left 12 million dollars to the Catholic Church, the largest single donation ever up to that

time, and somehow, in spite of their ethical and moral standards, the Church found a way to accept it.

28) When a person uses a bomb to blow himself up he can be classified as a suicide bomber, but when his purpose is to kill innocent people by that act and he's successful, to me that makes him a homicide bomber.

29) A lousy boss may outrank you, but that doesn't make him your superior; in fact, he's probably not even your equal.

30) Money may buy acceptance but never culture or class.

31) Americans now enjoy Ultimate Fighting Championships in much the same way as Romans enjoyed gladiator combat just before *their* empire started going down the tubes.

32) Teachers, displeased over contract talks or terms, decide to go on strike. Fine—but have you ever known any to do so during the summer or over a weekend?

33) I tuned in near the end of the 11th hour news, and some guy with maps behind him said he expected fewer showers after midnight. Well, of course—most working people have already showered and are asleep by then.

34) These days it seems that the only noteworthy thing to ever come out of a meeting after it's over are its participants.

35) It doesn't matter whether you plant a vegetable garden, a flower garden or a bluegrass lawn; in almost no time each will be overtaken by weeds, which makes me wonder: what would you wind up with if you planted weeds?

Chapter 14 –

Extreme Makeover Needed

You've gotten this far; your patience is admirable. Obviously, a book like this could go on indefinitely (so many topics, any one of which could be expanded into its own novel!), but we're getting there—just a few more topics to address which must be brought to your attention because they're important. They affect all of us and have the same common basis: each is a steadily worsening national problem that's being denied, minimized or ignored by a country that has become either hypnotized by "15-minutes-of-fame" scandals involving steroids, sex and drugs or is too self-absorbed, bipolar, pussyfied or jesusified to care.

There must be things that are of concern to you. They may be of national interest, such as global warming, the ethanol craze, violent video games, the vanishing middle class, the decline of excellence, taste or originality in the arts—again, the list is endless. They may be local issues: school budgets, a needed library expansion, poorly maintained roads or bridges, a new shopping mall planned for two blocks from your house, and so on. The point is, *you* are the key; *you* must be the one to get involved. Select an issue that concerns you (which implies that you already have an opinion) and learn all you can about *both sides* by listening to what people have to say, watching other than your favorite TV news channel, searching the Internet and even reading "*Time*"-type magazines or newspapers. Whether your efforts reinforce or change your point of view doesn't matter: you cared and were prepared. Now you can be an educated participant on-line and verbally and, perhaps, make a difference.

At worst, you will at least have tried, and that's a great way to set a good example, increase self-esteem and sleep well at night.

New York's Finest?

I had driven a group of us into mid-town Manhattan to attend a concert. There were no available parking spaces on the block with the concert hall but there were some around the corner. I parked the car, the five of us got out and walked up and down, looking for any sign within that block that would prohibit parking. Not only were there none but we saw a policeman walking in our direction. We greeted him, pointed to the car and asked if where we were parked was okay. He looked up and down the block and said, "Do you see a sign saying that you can't park here?" "No, sir," we responded. "Well, then," he assured us, "you're fine." We thanked him and headed off to enjoy the concert.

At intermission, one of the guys in the group suggested we check on the car. "Why?" I asked. "Do you think someone stole it?"

"No," he said, uneasily, "but I know New York City cops, and I don't trust them."

"Ridiculous," I said, "but all right. Come on; I'll go with you."

We left the hall, walked down the block and turned the corner. The car was still there; we could see the trunk and taillights. We continued walking until we were alongside the front windshield, which had something under the wiper blade on the driver's side. Turned out to be a ticket, issued for parking illegally. There was no fighting it or getting around it; I wound up having to pay it. Seems that the friend's opinion of the city's cops had some validity.

That was my first encounter with "New York's Finest."

Manhattan used to have a two-color traffic signal at each corner, with the red light above the green. There was no middle "yellow" light to warn you that the green was about to disappear in favor of the red; the light simply went from green to red. The problem, though, was that when the red came on the green stayed on a second or two more, so that briefly both were lit. If you approached or entered an intersection when this happened, there was no way you could even move your right foot from the gas pedal to the brake pedal in time, much less stop. Technically you had gone through a red light and could be pulled over by a cop and given a ticket, which is exactly what happened to us once heading south on Broadway. He was parked in his car diagonally across the street, facing north, waiting. I explained about the light, even had him watch as it did it again, but it didn't matter—I had broken the law and there was no way in hell he was going to let me off with a mere warning.

Relating this experience to friends over the next few months, we learned we weren't alone. One guy even suggested that the next time we drive through Manhattan we look for police cars parked on corners, with a cop sitting in the driver's seat. He was right; one could spot them every few blocks except occasionally when one would lurch forward with lights flashing, make a U-turn and pull over a car that had just gone through a red light.

That was my second experience with New York City police.

A few weeks before my first wife and I were to move out of our Manhattan apartment we both arrived home from work to find the door slightly ajar. Sure enough, someone had managed somehow to get in and burglarize the place. After carefully determining that it was safe to enter, we did; I called the police, and we waited.

Minutes later there was a cautious knock on the door. I opened it, but the expected policeman turned out to be a Latina who gave me a startled look and took off. I recovered and chased her down the hall to the stairs, even going down a couple of flights, but lost her. Somehow, she had simply vanished. I returned to our place.

Luckily there was no damage, so we began to take inventory. In checking the front closet I noticed that a white box which had been on a shelf was now lying on the floor, with its dusty top next to it. Within the dust were fingerprints that didn't belong to either of us.

Hours later two detectives in suits showed up. After answering their questions about how we discovered we had been robbed, what was taken and was there any damage they stopped writing and were getting ready to leave when I asked them to please stay a moment. I was curious, I said, about how anyone got in, since there wasn't any damage to the door lock—almost as if the building's superintendent had let them in. Maybe there were fingerprints on the doorknob. They both smiled. I then related the incident with the Latina, whom I said I could describe somewhat and who may also have left prints. They listened and nodded, again taking no notes or saying anything. Finally I opened the front closet door, right next to where they were standing, and showed them the box with its top. "Look at this top," I said, frustrated. "It's full of fingerprints that aren't ours. Don't you at least want to take it and maybe check them out?"

The detective nearest to me patted my shoulder. "Son," he said, grinning, "you've been watching too many TV shows." With that, the two detectives wished us good luck, said goodnight and left.

Luckily, that was the last time I had to deal with New York City police, and things have only deteriorated. The number of incidents involving ineptitude, incompetence, dishonesty or worse on their part appears to increase steadily, yet few are uncovered or reported and when they are, rarely are the involved cops prosecuted, much less found guilty, even if deadly encounters have occurred. If you have doubts, just watch the news on TV or read the papers.

Or go to the city yourself sometime.

Separating The Sheep From The Goats In The Shearing Room

When I was graduated from high school I wanted to be a teacher, but I knew that was impossible because it would interfere some day with a few of my hobbies, like being able to eat and pay rent. So I gave it up for career purposes but never abandoned the idea because I liked interacting with people, which was the reason I'd wanted to teach in the first place.

To set the record straight let me say here that with the exception of great parents there is probably nothing more important to future generations than a great teacher, a truly dedicated educator. This is not to minimize the importance of other professionals—certainly a fireman or doctor whose actions in a crisis save your life cannot be slighted—but chances are that their competent effectiveness is a product of either good upbringing, education or both. In addition to good parenting I was fortunate to have had some fine teachers and, as a "docent" working for years with classes of elementary-school students, to have been able to work with literally hundreds of grade-school teachers. As one would expect in any profession, most were good in varying degrees but not outstanding; the rest were split between superb and, to put it kindly, dreadful. What concerns me, though, is the steady change I've seen over the years in percentages, causing the bell-shaped curve of normalcy to shift to the left: the low end. Simply put, the number of lousy teachers is increasing at the expense of the ordinary and, worse yet, the great.

And it's becoming ever easier to single them out because there's more involved than just lower levels of student achievement, class control or alertness and enthusiasm. I think these people probably got into the profession because they knew they'd never be able to make it in the real world and this was the one field where they could reap the best benefits for producing poor products based on the lowest investment in time and effort. In other words, it beat working for a living at a full-time job and being held accountable for their work. But is this something they appreciate and silently accept with gratitude? Far from it. I can't tell you how many times I've overheard group discussions among them, and they're always the same: all one hears is bitching about their problems which, to them, with their limited insight into the business world, of course far exceed those of anyone else in any other job. It goes without saying that any outsider who points out something that weakens or negates these arguments is considered to be uninformed, unaware of system complexities (for example: "Yes, but you don't understand; you don't have to deal with the principal or our school board") or simply prejudiced.

Please remember: I'm talking here only about the low end of the profession, so let's take a look at some of these most oft-bitched-about complaints (not necessarily in order of importance):

Gripe 1: "We have a bad principal."

Response: I can sympathize with that, but he or she is your *only* boss. He isn't in the middle of a chain of command that includes a few executives above him and a string of assistant managers or supervisors below him but still above you, any of whom can pull rank or exercise authority in something involving you or your work. I'm also pretty certain that the principal doesn't get together with you several times a week to check on your progress or to present you with new data that will necessitate changes in your lesson plan, adding to your work load. But best of all, when you're in class, *you* are the boss; anyone who disobeys you or makes your life miserable can be sent to the principal's office for discipline or even possible suspension. You can also smile or say something nice to a student without having to worry about being accused of sexual harassment the next day.

Gripe 2: "We have to answer to the school board."

Response: Why is that of concern? If you have tenure, you can't be fired unless you do something illegal and the police have to be called. In the real world workers have to worry about the firm's executive board, and there's more: how about investors, shareholder meetings and the threat of a hostile takeover by a larger, uncaring company? How about a project leader in a family-owned company who has to worry about job security now that the CEO's son just got his college degree in Business Management?

Gripe 3: "I have to create a lesson plan."

Response: Unless this is your first year as a teacher or you teach 21st Century History, how often do you have to revise a lesson plan for such static subjects as English, math or biology, and even if you do, how long does it take? If it's that complicated or arduous, then think how lucky you are—you've got all summer to do it.

Gripe 4: "I have test papers to grade" (or homework to check).

Response: Yes, but tests are not given every day, and not all homework requires written papers or reports to be turned in; many involve reading or studying parts of textbooks for discussion and elaboration the next day in class. Besides, you can start grading or checking once you're home which, in many cases, can be as early as 3:30 P.M., since not too many of you have to spend three or more hours a day commuting. Today, it's common in business for a white-collar company "professional" (a programmer or a manager, engineer, etc.) to work beyond 6:00 P.M. and get home after 7:00 with work still to be done, due tomorrow. Oh, I almost forgot: if you're a high school teacher you probably monitor a "study hall," in which case you certainly have an opportunity while sitting for about 48 minutes to do some of that grading or checking.

Gripe 5: "Classes are too large—just too many students. There should never be more than 20 kids in a classroom."

Response: For special-ed classes, yes, but outside of that, no. I never had fewer than 25 classmates throughout school; in fact, I can recall one college chemistry class that was held in the auditorium because we numbered 110! Of the many class tours I conducted as a volunteer the only ones with fewer than 20 students were those whose members were home-schooled. Some "regular" schools sent classes with over 35 kids each and, without exception (I swear) they were the best, led by the cream-of-the-crop top level of teachers, fully prepared and in control, eight out of 10 of whom were women.

Gripe 6: "There's always so much to do; this is a stressful job."

Response: Compared to what? It's rare that you have to work more than three weeks without at least one day off, thanks to a holiday, snow day, winter break, spring recess, storm damage, last-minute bomb threat and probably more that I've overlooked. And given a typical day you're in school about seven hours, including lunch. You probably have a "teacher's aide" (talk about low pay!) and/or a parent volunteer to assist you, even if only for an hour or so each day. If you're out sick for a day or two a substitute takes over and keeps things going. If any white-collar worker is out sick for a couple of days she's lucky if her desk is just as she left it; usually it's piled high with more work, e-mail or phone messages to be answered that lead to more work, or both. You also don't face the problem of being assigned some or all of the work of a fellow worker who's been laid off—in other words, having your workload practically doubled with no increase in pay. If you can't cope, no one's forcing you to stay; try an office or factory job. If that's still too much for you to deal with, try being a waitress in a popular diner or cleaning baths and bedrooms in a motel.

Gripe 7: "We teachers aren't paid enough."

Response: This is the one that really irks me. Sure, there are parts of the nation in which teachers earn less than in the New York City area, but correspondingly it costs less to live in those places. But regardless of where you live, let's look at some things that you people seem to ignore and certainly never bring up in conversation.

You work less than half a year—180 days at most, even fewer if you take your sick days and personal days which, if not used, accumulate over the years and can be applied towards early retirement. "Professionals" typically put in at least 230 days (5 days a week for 52 weeks a year would be 260, but 10 vacation days, up to 10 holidays and 10 sick/personal days reduces it to 230). On average, most of them take less than two weeks vacation even if they're entitled to three or four weeks, and even fewer use up all of their sick or personal days which, in nearly all companies, are lost if not used within the year.

You and your family enjoy total medical coverage that doesn't cost you a penny in premiums or benefit co-payments. Not only are all your medical, dental, ophthalmologic, pharmaceutical, hospital and psychiatric needs paid for but after 25 years in your job you're covered for the rest of your life, again at no cost to you. Just in premium payments alone, how many hundreds of dollars has that saved you and your family *each month*, and what does that add up to over 25 years? About a quarter of a million dollars would be my guess, give or take. But more important, you're covered fully; not bad when you consider that just one blood transfusion that used to cost $25 not too many years ago can now run you $6,000!

You work under a contract that guarantees you a raise each year for three years. True, the amount may be only a small percentage of your salary—say, three per cent—but it's guaranteed, not an option. You have no idea how many workers in other professions haven't had a raise in three or more years. And inseparably connected to that: you have tenure. It may have taken you three years and one day of good behavior and sucking up to your boss to achieve it but once you did you were protected and, as I indicated before, there's virtually no way to get rid of you now. How many other workers, union or non-union, single or married, good or bad, have that kind of security, even after 30 years and one day? I can remember as a youngster in the 1940s hearing a few teachers complain about their low salaries, perhaps justifiably so, but I also remember my father wryly reminding them how quiet they were during the Great Depression of the 1930s.

You get a pension, which by the time you retire (even if you opt for early retirement) can amount to as much as 75 per cent of the salary you earned in your last year or two. I'll let you do the math.

By the way, my earliest trips to Europe were made with friends who were teachers—in fact, my first wife and I were the only ones in the group each year who were not in the profession or members of the NEA (National Education Association), through whom these trips were arranged. If teachers in general are paid so little how can they do so much traveling, whether during winter or spring breaks or for as much as an entire summer? How come I've never run into a teacher who lives in the slums of any town or city? And how can so many retire at age 55?

Some of you point out that you work longer hours because you coach sports, tutor or teach summer school. Sorry, but that's paid work, not volunteering. I can accept coaching but the other two vex me: if you and your colleagues are so good why do those kids need additional or corrective education? If you couldn't do your job in nine months how will a few more hours or days improve anything for them (another reason I'm so adamantly opposed to tenure)?

There probably are many other things that could be pointed out or discussed (I haven't even gotten into sabbaticals), but let me end with this thought: just remember that you're through with those malleable impressionable "problem students" in June, having carried them for nine months without bettering them. Years later, when they're set in their ways, *we* have to deal with them in the real world for the remainder of their working lives unless they join your profession, in which case the future of your legacy is assured.

In short, make no mistake: there's a big difference between a teacher and someone who's nothing more than a white-collar union worker with a blue-collar mentality.

Will The Reverend Never Bend Or Ever End?

Civil rights activist Reverend Al Sharpton lashed out for years against perceived injustices against blacks, and soon had listeners nationwide realizing that his principles applied to all, regardless of race or religion. People even dismissed a few factual inaccuracies and believed him until the Tawana Brawley farce of 1987, in which her rape claim against several white men proved to be totally false. Still, his outspoken support of her never wavered, nor did he ever apologize, but then there was more: Jessie Jackson's "Hymietown" comment, Louis Farrakan's frequent and scathing anti-Semitic speeches and, worst of all, the murder in Brooklyn of a visiting Australian Orthodox Jewish student, Yankel Rosenbaum, by a group of blacks in retaliation for the accidental running down of a black man by another Orthodox Jew in a car, which they perceived as a deliberate racial attack. For all these offenses and many others by blacks against Jews he remained silent and still does to this day, unchallenged by other famous blacks or Jews or Liberals, which is why I'm disappointed with them all—but not surprised.

Chapter 15 –

Gratitude Without Platitude

It's your first time ever at a major-league baseball stadium. It's exciting being a part of the action, joining the grownups around you as they stand in waves and cheer for the home team—not at all like watching it on television. You're enjoying this game even more because your team is ahead and there's been lots of action. It's also a beautiful, sunny day and you just finished a delicious hot dog and ice-cold soda you got from a shouting vendor going up and down the stairs. It's a memorable day, and even though you're sharing it with 55,000 other people, it's special to you.

And then comes the eighth inning, and that's when it happens: a pitch that your favorite batter just connected with is flying towards your section of the bleachers. Reactions are mixed—a few people just sit and watch; some actually duck or put their arms in front of their faces to protect themselves; a few even lean in the direction of the ball and stick out their hands, hoping to catch it. But the ball is curving towards you, and you were smart enough to bring your mitt. Quickly you stand, reach up over your right shoulder with your left hand and jump. Incredibly, you're successful—the home run ball your hero just hit is yours. You're applauded and congratulated by the people around you, which is almost a bit embarrassing, but this event has changed the significance of the day for you. In addition to having acquired a meaningful souvenir and an even more intense love for the national pastime, you now stand out from everyone else there. The day has changed from being one that you might think of occasionally to one you'll remember with pride and never forget. You tried something daring and succeeded, and that's given you the basis for a story that only you can recount from your vantage point and share with others. That one event—that catch—is what makes the story exclusively yours.

Which is why, occasionally, you should take a moment or so to appreciate some of those memorable or outstanding good things you've enjoyed or that have influenced your life up to this point, along with those noteworthy blessings that continue to be part of your life each day, and share them with others, to give them something to think about.

My Favorite Lines Of Poetry

America, America,
God shed his grace on thee.
And crown thy good with brotherhood,
From sea to shining sea.

The President Was Right, And So Am I

Former President Harry Truman thought he was a very fortunate man. Although he had experienced much—fame, travel, luxury—he was at his happiest back home in Missouri, which he considered the best place to be, continuing to enjoy an unpretentious lifestyle with Bess, the lady he regarded as the ideal wife with whom to share a life they both loved. He was right: he was lucky, and so is anyone else who finds such contentment in life. I have no desire to live in Missouri and I know many people who wouldn't live here in New York State if you paid them, but that's the way it should be—whatever works to make one happy. I can relate to the President's feelings because he had his Bess and I have my Barbara. Thanks to her we have exactly the kind of life we want where we want it, and sharing it with her makes me one of the luckiest guys in the world. How wonderful a person is she, and how magical has she made our life together? I wish I could share that with you but so far no one—not even Webster, Shakespeare or Mozart—has created the words or music I'd need to even begin to describe the extent of either.

Rediscover The Lost Generations Of Musicians

Of the many interests in which I became passionately involved as a youngster—from reading and photography to playing softball and riding river rapids on an inner tube—none affected my life more profoundly than music. I grew up with music from around the world: folk, jazz, rhythm and blues, dance, popular orchestral and vocal, country, even cartoon soundtracks, but classical music most touched my soul. I couldn't get enough, and the more I explored that world the more I found to listen to and learn. Improvements in engineering and technology—magnetic tape, long-playing records, compact discs—created a musical world of unimaginable size and quality. As a result, over the years I've heard countless works by hundreds of composers performed by hundreds of artists. Naturally, one can't help but favor certain ones over others and want to share these preferences with other classical music lovers, but that creates a problem: as with religion or politics, opinions can be controversial (does Wilhelm Bachaus play Grieg's *Piano Concerto* better than Walter Gieseking?).

Please bear with me: I know how I feel when I read some current self-proclaimed music critic's list of "One Hundred Essential Pieces of Classical Music" or "The Top 100 Classical Recordings" (which rarely if ever includes any artists born before 1960, by the way). If you love classical or any other form of music I'm sure you could create your own list; any music lover could, and I'd be truly surprised if any two of them had more than five choices in common.

But there is that pinnacle achieved by just a few in any form of music, artists whose talents far exceeded the meteoric moment of fame from one or two hit records. Their artistry was extraordinary enough to keep them at the top for years. Unfortunately, too many are now being ignored or overlooked. Put simply, many inimitable musicians from the past are being forgotten, lost to a world of lower standards of excellence that seems to have dismissed the importance of creativity or individuality and passion in music. Sticking with classical music, what I've done here is to select just two artists (out of how many?) that deserve to be marveled at today. If you're a music lover I hope that you will enjoy rediscovering or perhaps discovering these and others, and keep their talents alive.

As Samuel L. Goldwyn might have creatively observed, "There are more pianists in heaven and earth, Horatio, than you can shake a stick at." And he'd probably be right. Once the modern piano as we know it replaced the clavichord and harpsichord in the latter half of the 19th century its popularity increased, leading to more students and performers. The introduction of the phonograph record in the early 20th century and radio in the 1920s created a global audience of music lovers as well as a Golden Age of Piano that lasted into the 1940s. These years saw many fine pianists and a few outstanding ones, like Josef Hofmann, Sergei Rachmaninoff, Artur Rubinstein and Vladimir Horowitz, still remembered today. But most are now forgotten, including the 20th century's most unique and gifted one.

His name was Simon (pronounced "See-moan") Barere, born in Russia in 1896 to a poor family. Although his pianistic gifts were acknowledged early, circumstances throughout his life created what was almost a preordained destiny guaranteed to prevent sustained international fame until the end of the second World War, when his fortunes began to change. Sadly, though, fate triumphed; Barere died in 1951 on-stage in Carnegie Hall while in performance with The Philadelphia Orchestra, led by Eugene Ormandy.

Fortunately for us Barere's legacy survives through recordings, most made during live concerts in Carnegie Hall by his son, Boris. All have been restored, released as boxed sets of multiple compact discs by Appian Publications & Recordings (APR), England. While all are very much worth listening to a few selections are incredible enough to highlight here, since they best demonstrate how his gifts, equaled by his unique understanding of the pieces, enabled him to overcome their difficulties and present the real hidden music. No one could equal Barere's abilities on these selections; in some cases no other pianist even tried to perform them. And don't forget: these were live recordings, made under the stress of performance before a concert audience, on acetate records. There was no "Take 2" or, in those days, magnetic tape to use snippets of after multiple attempts back at the studio to try and produce a decent version of the piece. All of his recordings are on CD (e.g., CDAPR 7001, CDAPR 7007, 7008 and 7009). I've chosen just five that I hope you will try to listen to. Frankly, I think you'll be both moved and astounded:

1) Schumann: Toccata in C, Opus 7
2) Liszt: Rapsodie espagnole, S. 254
3) Blumenfeld: Etude for the Left Hand
It took being in Carnegie Hall and seeing Barere play this in person for the music world to believe it was even possible.
4) Balakirev: Islamey – Oriental fantasie
Even Balakirev, a pianist himself, couldn't play this piece!
5) Chopin: Ballade No. 1 in G Minor, Opus 23
This is the only one of the five not recorded in concert; it displays the true Barere, the consummate musician.

Unlike the world of piano, there are far fewer notable violinists. In the early 20th century there were barely a dozen, including Pablo de Sarasate, Jan Kubelik, Fritz Kreisler, Mischa Elman, Josef Szigeti and Efram Zimbalist, Sr. In the 1920s fresh new artists, led by Jascha Heifetz, began to attract attention, and in the 1930s a new group of worthies had risen to the top— almost. Although gifted, they were overshadowed by Heifetz, whose total skills elevated him to the top spot as the king of string, a position he held for years. To enjoy continued recognition and appreciation the others had to showcase their special talents to attract and maintain loyal admirers. Each succeeded, but only one surpassed the others.

Yehudi Menuhin was a true child prodigy. Born in 1916 in New York City, he began violin studies at age four, gave his first concert at age seven and made his Carnegie Hall debut with the New York Philharmonic, performing the Beethoven *Violin Concerto* at age 10! His appeal became global as he mastered those intuitive gifts that gave him the ability to project warmth and excitement, form perfect phrases with varied shades of vibrato and masterful bowmanship, and create music rather than merely surpass technical demands. He played with sentiment but not sentimentality, emotion but not "schmaltz," passion and a refreshing sense of spontaneity.

His best recordings of the classics were made in the 1930s, at the height of his formative years. Of the many concertos and short works recorded for RCA Victor (or HMV) all have been remastered digitally and released as CDs by EMI Records. I've selected just three that, to me, are the best examples of Menuhin's genius:

1) Mendelssohn: Violin Concerto in E minor, Opus 64
(Orchestre des Concerts Colonne; Georges Enesco, conductor)
More than playing; Menuhin sings and speaks Mendelssohn.
2) Lalo: Symphonie Espagnole, Opus 21
(Symphony Orchestra of Paris; Georges Enesco, conductor)
No one else even comes close—and it's unabridged.
3) Paganini: Violin Concerto No. 1 in D Major, Opus 6
(Paris Symphony Orchestra; Pierre Monteux, conductor)
You could dance to the first movement, and at the end of the
Sauret cadenza you'll have goose bumps—it's incredible!

One more observation to share, if I may. Of course, there's a lot of classical music to love and enjoy, and we probably all have a few that are our favorites. But if I had to select just one composition as my top choice it would definitely be the "Incidental Music to *A Midsummer Night's Dream*," Opp. 21 & 61 by Felix Mendelssohn. I especially love the *Overture*, written when Mendelssohn was only 16 years old. Properly performed, it evokes images of the nostalgic best of the Romantic era, from softly whispering leafy branches to dreamy, heavenly cherubs and other celestial or ethereal images.

There are many recordings of this work, some complete but most abridged—that is, they contain only the most popular excerpts from the complete work, which is fine: quality should always supercede quantity, but "properly performed" really narrows the field. To me, the best version of this work (and, in my opinion, one of the most near-perfect interpretations and performances of any work) was one made in performance in Carnegie Hall early in November, 1947 by the NBC Symphony Orchestra, directed by Arturo Toscanini. What makes it so marvelous is the perfect pace at which it's played (not too fast, not too slow), the astonishing synchronization of the string section (all playing as one) and the dynamic range of the orchestra, from wispy, almost tenuous subtlety to impassioned fortitude and strength. My one lament: I wish it had "You spotted snakes," an excerpt included in a 1942 recording with Toscanini conducting the Philadelphia Orchestra (a nice performance, by the way, but I still prefer the 1947 version). Fortunately, both were recorded and have been digitally restored and issued as RCA Gold Seal CDs.

To answer the old question: if I had to be marooned on a desert island with just one recording, but it could be any one I picked, the CD containing this 1947 version of my favorite composition would be my choice. Of course, I'd have to hope that I'd be stranded with a CD player that could run on solar power, not electricity.

Harry Levy

We were almost through a short story in our sixth-grade reader from which students had been selected to read a paragraph or two aloud. It had been difficult at times for some of us to sit through this because a few were poor readers, but we soon learned to control our fidgeting. After all, some were immigrants, striving to master our language, and they were succeeding. We could see the progress over a few weeks as Mr. Levy worked patiently and diligently with them. The story ended and we knew it must be getting close to nine o'clock because he glanced at his watch, nodded and walked over to the large radio. Turning his head towards us he smiled and asked, invitingly, "Shall we listen to *The Masterwork Hour*?" As usual, everyone responded affirmatively with nods, yesses and applause. He then turned on the radio, already set to WNYC, the city's public station, and we began to enjoy an hour of classical music.

Each school day began this way at P.S. 179 in Manhattan unless there had been a problem with one or more students the day before, the punishment for which was the loss of the program we all looked forward to hearing the next day. Faced with our united disapproval and criticism for the rest of the day, such errant behavior on the part of those few miscreants soon virtually vanished.

Harry Levy was a gentle, soft-spoken man with distinctive facial features that I thought resembled those of Henry Clay, except our teacher was much more handsome. Blessed with communication skills he never spoke to us in a condescending manner but as equals, magically able to evoke enthusiastic participation in discussions and challenges. When he would point to one of several colored sheets of paper running across the top of three of the classroom walls and ask a student what the four numbers "1513" on it represented, you just knew that the student would provide the correct response: "Balboa discovered the Pacific Ocean." Anyone could recite the multiplication tables from "1 times 1 is 1" through "12 times 12 is 144" and, more impressively, quickly answer such direct challenges as "7 times 8," "19 minus 12," "16 plus 13"or "77 divided by 11." Tin came from Bolivia, coffee from Colombia; Lima was the capital of Peru, and all three countries were in South America. Many of us knew Rudyard Kipling's poem *"If"* by heart or could recite *"Abou ben Adhem"* by Leigh Hunt. Every correct response was rewarded with praise, given freely and sincerely. You were always proud of yourself as well as your fellow classmates. What a team we were!

Mr. Levy was also in charge of audio-visual equipment for the school and for obtaining films requested by other teachers, which sometimes provided us with opportunities to see fine short films in our classroom. It was there that I first saw the exquisitely-animated 1936 M-G-M "Happy Harmonies" color cartoon *"To Spring,"* with its beautiful accompanying soundtrack, and the 1945 Special Oscar-winning Frank Sinatra classic short *"The House I Live In,"* which offered a wartime plea for racial, religious and ethnic tolerance, very appropriate for our diverse class. There were others, of course, but I never forgot those two, whose merits we discussed afterwards.

There's one other thing I'd like to tell you about. The borough of Brooklyn had its own public radio station WNYE, an affiliate of Manhattan's WNYC. One of the things they aired during the day included a live "quiz show" competition between several public schools (unfortunately I don't remember the name of the show or its broadcast schedule). One morning Mr. Levy informed us that our school was soon going to participate and that someone from our class was to represent the school. Then he announced that I had been selected to be that one contestant.

The day of the contest found me sitting at a rectangular table in a small studio at WNYE's broadcast facilities. To my left were a few competitors and some more across the table, facing us. A genial announcer, standing at the head of the table, briefed us about how the show would work: he would ask a question, and anyone who knew the answer would raise their hand and wait for him to call on the first one who did. He reminded us that this was being broadcast and asked us to please keep things quiet except when called upon to respond. Glancing at the clock on the wall he picked up his microphone, turned his head and looked at the man behind the glass in the engineering booth, who soon nodded and pointed at him and, with that signal, the program began.

There were many varied questions asked and answered, but as it got towards the end all of us knew that it was a close contest. Then the announcer informed us that for our last challenge we were going to hear a musical selection that we were to identify. With that, the piece began. After the third note my hand shot up. He saw it, put his index finger to his lips and began shaking his head slightly, urging me to wait until more had been played. After a few seconds he called on me; I responded with, "The '*Gold and Silver*' waltz," which was correct. As it turned out, that answer made our school the winner and me, back in class the next day, a hero.

I was fortunate enough to have had other wonderful instructors over the years but none that could approach Harry Levy's talent and ability to successfully get the best out of each student in a class with so many different backgrounds and varying abilities. He created an environment in which learning was as exciting and rewarding as winning a game of curb-ball or stoopball. He had the gift, and he used it to teach students, not subjects.

Towards the end of the school year, as was the custom, we classmates exchanged autographs. It was a time of mixed emotions because this was our last year in public school; seventh grade would necessitate us all beginning junior high school at another location. For me that would be across the Hudson River, in New Jersey, to which we were moving within days. I approached Mr. Levy's desk and waited for the two girls ahead of me to obtain his signature, then asked if he would please sign my autograph book. He smiled, said "Certainly" and took the small book. He looked at the blank page, thought for a couple of seconds, then tilted the book slightly to the left and began to print:

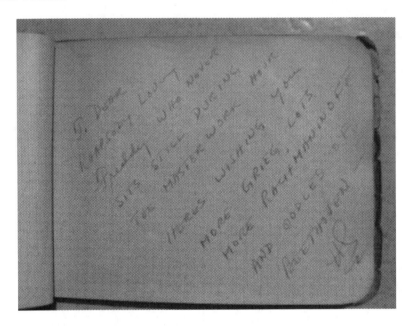

One Good Turner Deserves Another

Newton Minnow described television as "a vast wasteland"—and that was in its Golden Age, the days of maybe a dozen available channels operating for half a day, providing unsteady transmission to unreliable small-screen sets with no cable, color, stereo or high definition. But a 1-hour show meant over 54 minutes of substance.

One evening in May, 2008 Barbara had to attend a meeting and would have missed the season's final episode of *"Boston Legal,"* so I taped it for both of us to enjoy the following night. When it ended I thought that it seemed to have been rather short, but I attributed my perception to the ability to "fast-forward" past the commercials. I knew that out of 60 minutes of time allotted to such shows you're lucky to get 44 to 45 minutes of actual program content. Still, I felt something was strange, so I decided to check it out the next day.

I wasn't wrong; the actual episodic content was only 40 minutes. The other 20 presented endless repetitive drug and car commercials and promos for up-and-coming shows. Even within the "good" 40 minutes, more promos designed to catch your eye (and larger than last week's) continued to intrude every few minutes in the lower left-hand corner of the screen, with the station's permanent logo to the right. At the end the illegible credits raced up from the bottom quarter of the screen, overshadowed by a "coming up next" promo.

About six weeks later Disney Channel showed *"Camp Rock,"* a 2008 movie that began at 8:00 P.M. and ended before 9:45, with a few breaks—barely 1¾ hours. The very next night ABC Television (owned, incidentally, by Disney) showed *the same movie*. It began at 8:00 P.M. and was over *at 11:00 P.M.—3 hours!*

And these were but two shows on two channels, out of hundreds. Just try to imagine what TV will be like five or ten years from now. It's almost enough to give it up, except that there are a few channels out there—maybe a dozen—that still respect viewers and try to get them involved, to entertain and educate them in spite of Madison Avenue. They're good, but one really stands out above the others. In my opinion it's the best channel on television. It's called Turner Classic Movies (TCM), for which I gratefully thank Ted Turner.

Having achieved incredible success with several cable channels and mergers, he was able to purchase and secure the rights to the M-G-M film library and set out on a mission to preserve and restore the films, acquire more and make them available for viewing to the television audience—complete, uninterrupted and commercial-free. To say he succeeded doesn't begin to describe the enormity of his efforts. Literally, much of the world of silent cinema, forgotten or presumed lost even by experts, was rediscovered and restored, as were many relatively recent films that were starting to decay. Now, thanks in large part to Mr. Turner's initiatives and ongoing efforts, many other individuals and organizations have become involved, and because of them, over 100 years of films, shorts, cartoons, specials (and yes—even original promos!) can now be enjoyed and appreciated on TCM. How nice to be able to relive the days of class, style, elegance, music, humor and more! One might even think of it as born-again cinema.

He may not have been included in any *Time* magazine annual list of "100 Most Influential People," but I truly think that the cinematic world and its admirers should regard Ted Turner as a savior.

Take A Minute To Think About That Minute

It had not been the best day at work but at least it was over. Joe could hardly wait to get home, relax and forget about the lousy sales figures the place had suffered for the fourth month in a row. At this rate he'd be out of a job in five or six weeks. Well, he'd get home and...ah, nuts—he had to stop to get milk. Damn; why couldn't he just head home? Couldn't she have picked some up earlier? He got to the store, parked and went inside, got a gallon container and went to the register to pay for it. There was only one person ahead of him, and the clerk had just finishing ringing up her few items. The lady had her credit card ready and swiped it; it didn't take. She looked at it, then at the clerk, who told her to try again. She did; same result. Joe could feel his blood pressure rising. What's with these goddamned crap boxes? At that point the clerk realized what was happening and suggested that she try again but this time turn the card around so that the magnetic strip went through the slot. It worked; she was able to sign the slip, gather up her stuff and leave. Joe forced himself to keep quiet. Stupid-ass moron—it was her fault, not the machine's. What a jackass. He really needed this *agita* after the day he'd had. He paid for the milk in cash and was soon back in his car, ready to continue home.

Heading home he turned on the radio and found some soothing music. He soon realized just how wound up he'd been and made a conscious effort to relax. He thought about the woman in the store and almost started to laugh. Boy, he must really have been uptight. That poor lady; good thing he'd kept his mouth shut. So she made a mistake—big deal. How much time did he lose, maybe 30 seconds? Big deal. Don't sweat the small stuff, Joe, he told himself. He soon left the town road, joined Route 80 and was starting to feel good when he heard a crashing sound. He didn't know what or where it was but then he began seeing brake lights not too far ahead, causing both lanes going in his direction to slow down to a crawl. It wasn't long before traffic came to a complete halt, but he was close enough to see what had happened. Apparently an SUV heading in the other direction had lost control, crossed the grass divider and crashed into a car in his lane. Drivers nearer to the scene were getting out to see if they could help. Joe wasn't that close, but close enough to see that it didn't look good; there might even be fatalities. Wow, he thought, I really lucked out. I mean, hey, that could have been my car. What if I'd left work just a few seconds earlier? Or driven a little faster?

And then it hit him, and he paled. Maybe the Lord does work in mysterious ways.

What if that lady had swiped her card correctly the first time?

A Final Thought

It began as a youngster spending summers at my folks' country home and continued for an even longer period of time living in the suburbs, at first with them and then as part of my own life. Now, more than half a dozen decades later I'm back living year-round in the country—with Barbara, true, but that one aspect of my life that began when I was a kid hasn't changed and, hopefully, won't until the end, which is how I know exactly what to put on my tombstone:

"At Last! Someone Else to Mow the Lawn!"